YOU HAVE TO BE WILLING TO

DIE

DON'T BE
MOVED BY
WHAT YOU
HEAR

YOU HAVE TO BE WILLING TO

WILLING TO

DIE

DON'T BE MOVED BY WHAT YOU HEAR

LINDA WIMES

You Have To Be Willing to Die:
Don't Be Moved by What You Hear

Copyright © 2020 Linda Wimes

Unless otherwise noted, all Scripture quotations are from THE HOLY BIBLE, NEW INTERNATIONAL VERSION ®. Copyright© 1973, 1978, 1984, 2011 by Biblica, Inc.™. Used by permission of Zondervan. All rights reserved.

Scriptures marked AMP are taken from the AMPLIFIED® BIBLE, Copyright © 1954, 1958, 1962, 1964, 1965, 1987 by the Lockman Foundation Used by Permission. (**www.Lockman.org**)

Scriptures marked KJV are taken from the KING JAMES VERSION (KJV): KING JAMES VERSION, public domain.

Scripture marked MSG are taken from THE MESSAGE, Copyright © 1993, 2002, 2018 by Eugene H. Peterson. Used by permission of NavPress. All rights reserved. Represented by Tyndale House Publishers, Inc.

Published by Linda Wimes
P.O. Box 10025
Dothan, AL 36304

ISBN: 978-0-578-80156-8

Cover and Interior Design by Ebony Horton
Printed in the United States of America

DISCLAIMER

This book is not meant to be used, nor should it be used, to diagnose or treat any medical condition. For diagnosis or treatment of any medical problem, consult your own physician.

DEDICATIONS

This book is dedicated to all who need hope and encouragement. It's to those of you who see no way out, and those of you who have been told nothing else can be done and you feel like giving up.

This book is also dedicated to my children who I have come to love as mine with my involvement with HIS Prison Ministries. You did not ask for the fate that life dealt you. You are so special to God and to us. You are not forgotten, and you are not alone. We love you.

TABLE OF CONTENTS

FOREWORD

Hearing my mom say the words, "They say I have cancer but I'm about to go shopping for my kids Christmas," left me feeling shocked, confused and hopeful all at the same time.

No one is ever fully prepared to hear a negative report, but there was something to how my mom responded that changed my life forever. I'll never forget being in my apartment getting the news but knowing that this was bigger than my attempts to worry. When I cried, my 5-pound baby love, Armani, made sure that I was comforted and didn't allow me to cry long. He forced me to get up and walk outside. I learned from him that I needed to do the same for my mom.

From my front row seat, I saw every physical change but never saw my mom's spirit or hope in God change. Constantly hearing her praise, worship, pray and cry out to God for others proved that this battle was not just for her.

In these moments, I learned how to pray, think good thoughts, surround myself with fighters and boldly reject anything that went against the Word of God.

As you read this book, my prayer is that you rest in knowing that God is madly in love with you. He allows your issues to work out for your good and to bring Him glory. You're a piece of His Master Plan that the world needs to see!

P.S. Grab a blanket, tissue, and some tea or coffee because reading this book is going to be a good ride!

~ Christi Wimes

FOREWORD

I had never walked with anyone through a cancer diagnosis before. When my wife, Linda, was diagnosed, it was closer to home than anything I expected. You see it with other people and how they go through it. You really don't know until it hits you what the journey will look like. This was my wife.

You will have to make a lot of adjustments. I prayed more than I normally do. I received God's Word and never felt like giving up. Going through this increased my faith. The walk I have with Him became stronger; my relationship with God was a lot more believable. It was because of this that I never saw a dying person, but rather a person who was going through some changes. I am confident that the pages you read in this book will show you the same thing, and show you that there's hope in God, no matter what you endure.

~ Fred Wimes

PREFACE

My story started around April 2007, when I discovered a small knot on my scalp. The doctor said, "It's a cyst." He provided treatment and said it should drain. I was scheduled to return in two days for a follow-up. Well, it did not drain and within hours had turned into a cutaneous abscess. A big lump appeared on the left side of my neck. My glands were swollen. I was terrified. My doctor didn't have any available appointments so I went to another doctor. This one said, "You have an ear infection." I left that office shaking my head.

When I returned to my doctor for the scheduled follow-up appointment, he was concerned and referred me to an ear, nose, and throat (ENT) doctor who was not able to see me until eight days later. That was way too long! It was beginning to appear that I was the only one with a sense of urgency. My wheels were spinning. I needed help.

I thought of another doctor I knew and went straightway to his office. He made an assessment and said the cyst may have to be excised (or surgically removed) if it was not better. I continued the antibiotics I was prescribed earlier and returned as instructed.

The cyst grew to 2.5 centimeters, about the size between the first knuckle of your thumb and your thumb tip. The entire lesion was excised and the results of the biopsy showed only "nonspecific inflammation" and an intradermal scar. The path was benign. My doctor felt the knot would go away. Within days, the area was finally healing.

Then, a new mass on the left side of my neck appeared. It was firm and measured four centimeters. A needle biopsy of the lesion showed only skeletal muscle with "focal mild nonspecific chronic inflammation." A CT scan of my neck showed a 3 x 2.5-centimeter left posterior triangle mass with adjacent inflammation with the evidence of necrosis. There was concern for neoplasm, such as squamous cells, but no real alarm for cancer. The mass was persistent, so my doctor and I agreed to get to the bottom of the situation.

I underwent surgery to remove the mass. Six days would pass before I knew the results. I was obviously feeling anxious. Can you imagine waiting any amount of time to find out what's going on with your body?

Day seven, September 4, 2007, came. Before my appointment, I sat in my bedroom praying and talking to the Lord. "Lord, I don't know what's going on and the doctors don't either," I said. I finished praying, sat quietly, and then I heard someone say "lymphoma." I looked around. I was supposed to be the only one in the house because my husband, Fred, was out of town.

Then, I immediately heard, "Don't be moved by what you hear." I knew who it was. Such a peace came over me. You have to experience God speaking to you for yourself to truly understand. But it happens. All of a sudden I was prepared, at peace, and wasn't going to be moved. I got dressed and went to my appointment.

I arrived at my appointment and was met with the news. "Linda, it's cancer," my doctor said. He later called and said, "It's lymphoma."

Lymphoma. That is the word I had heard while I was praying. The doctor's words were just the confirmation. "Okay, so where do we go from here?" I responded to the doctor. He referred me to a local oncologist. I went to the appointment two days later on September 6, 2007. After a long discussion, I received a referral to a specialist in Birmingham for a consultation.

On September 13, 2007, we arrived at my appointment with the specialist. He was very thorough, took the time to explain what was going on, and answered all of my questions (and I had lots of them). He wasn't in a hurry and seemed to care about my situation and about me. What was to be a referral turned into me choosing him as my actual doctor. He presented his plan of care: six to eight cycles of chemotherapy in three-week intervals and supported by Neulasta®. In addition, I was told that I needed therapy and that my prognosis would ultimately be fatal without treatment. Still, there was the most important disclaimer that there was no guarantee of success.

I asked if I could have another CT scan before I started the treatment. I can't explain why I asked. He agreed and it was performed on September 28, 2007. The CT scan of my neck showed bilateral cervical lymphadenopathy measuring approximately 1.5 centimeters, but no other adenopathy in the chest, abdomen, or pelvis.

Arrangements were made to return in ten days to initiate the first treatment. I returned on October 1, 2007. The doctor discussed the side effects of therapy, including nausea, vomiting, mucositis, alopecia, peripheral neuropathy, cardiomyopathy, myelosuppression, febrile neutropenia, bleeding, bruising, and blood transfusion. I was counseled on the risks of febrile neutropenia. He discussed monitoring the side effects, especially neuropathy.

I completed the first chemotherapy treatment with no problem. However, I had some side effects. I called my doctor and was told what to do to alleviate the pain. I returned on October 24, 2007, for my second treatment. I experienced more bone pains, several days of anxiety, and difficulty sleeping from the prednisone. I lost all of my hair, which was another expected side effect.

I talked to the Lord and decided to stop further treatments. Yes, *I stopped treatment*. I did not hear a voice telling me to stop treatment but I had such an unexplainable peace. I called my doctor's office and informed his nurse that I would no longer be taking chemo. She asked that I come as scheduled and discuss it with my doctor.

I returned on November 14, 2007, and informed my doctor of my decision. We had a lengthy discussion; he was clear about the implications regarding treatment, failure, and death from lymphoma. He noted:

Ms. Wimes has had an excellent clinical response to I think two cycles of CHOP chemotherapy, and clinically there is no residual disease. However, she does not like how she feels in chemotherapy, and does not want to take any more treatment. I had an extended conversation with her lasting greater than 50% of this 40-minute visit regarding the indication of the treatment. She certainly understands the implications of alternating therapy at this time, and notes that this is associated with a high-risk treatment failure, and obviously a high chance of compromising the survival. … I was clear with her about the implications regarding treatment failure and death from lymphoma, but she will not consider receiving more treatment at the moment. She is confident.

I knew the "risk involved" was death. I wasn't trying to die and I didn't want to die. I wanted to live. But I was willing to die. What did I have to lose? I think of that as a rhetorical question. I was never given a guarantee that the chemotherapy would cure me. The risk of losing peace and a quality of life was more than the idea of losing what little life the doctors were thinking I had left.

My doctor offered me some treatment adjustments. He discussed my switching to radiotherapy. He wasn't enthusiastic about it but felt this might give me a better chance than abandoning therapy altogether. I told him I would consider doing so. He asked that I return in two weeks and bring my family with me to discuss it.

Fred and I returned on November 28, 2007. My doctor noted:

She states she "would rather be dead" than have further treatment based on how poorly it made her feel, and the negative impact it is having on her work as a prison Minister. … I was quite clear with her about my concern that she has not had enough therapy to be cured. Despite the excellent clinical response to treatment, she remains at very high risk of recurrence of her disease. I also noted that T-cell lymphomas have a worse prognosis than B-cell lymphomas, and there has not been a good experience with abbreviated therapy. I also discussed with her the possibility of making changes in the chemotherapy regimen to try and make it more tolerable (e.g. stopping the prednisone) or switching to radiotherapy. She voiced a clear

understanding as to the risks that she is taking, and clearly voiced the
reasons for taking that risk, which is that she feels so terrible on
chemotherapy that she is not willing to go on with it.
Additionally, it is stopping her from doing very important work that
she has now and upcoming over the holidays. I stressed to her that she
is not making the right medical decision and that she may be putting
herself at risk of not being there for her family and colleagues in the
future and she understands that explicitly. Nevertheless she is unable
to proceed with therapy now.

Fred and I don't recall me telling my doctor, "I would rather be dead." I explained how I viewed healing and said, "I was willing to die for what I believed." God knows I wasn't trying to die. I know this may sound crazy, but I didn't have time to die at the moment. We were preparing for HIS Prison Ministries' Christmas Party for the children. We couldn't let them down. Our babies depended on us, and we looked forward to this event as much as they did.

I was beginning to feel like myself again within a month of the last chemo session. Then, two hair bumps appeared on the right side of my neck around February 11, 2008. My daughter, Shalunda, and I burst them. They became raised and hardened in about two days. I went to see a dermatologist on February 28, 2008, and she removed hair from the spots. The bumps didn't seem to be improving. This began to feel like déjà vu. I had traveled this road before.

I stayed calm and returned for my follow-up appointment on March 6, 2008, with the dermatologist. She performed a punch biopsy. Twelve days later, on March 18, 2008, I received a call from the dermatologist telling me the cancer had come back.

I told my regular doctor it was nothing and that the two hair bumps were like little peas. After our discussion, he told me to come to my regularly scheduled appointment on March 31, 2008. I went to my appointment. He asked me to show him what they were talking about. I did. He said, "Ms. Wimes, I don't feel anything." He noted:

Ms. Wimes appears to have relapsed ALCL CD 30 positive. It appears to be localized to the right neck, contralateral to her original presentation. Clinically there are no other sites of disease. She has not had re imaging studies performed. I spent the majority of this 30-minute visit in direct face to face discussion with the patient and her husband regarding prognosis and further management. Superficially she has a low disease burden. We will reimage her when she returns in two weeks' time with CT scans and a PET scan and also get a bone marrow biopsy. I again reviewed treatment options with her. Obviously, the prognosis will be guided by the extent of disease and response of therapy, but I feel she really must receive systemic chemotherapy followed by involved field radiotherapy. She will not consider receiving CHOP again because of how poorly it made her feel last year but would consider a different chemotherapy. I am not enthusiastic about radiation alone but have arranged for her to see Dr. Meredith this afternoon to review this option with her. … Ms. Wimes was surprisingly open minded about receiving therapy with the exception of CHOP because of how poorly she felt with it. She will see what Dr. Meredith has to say. … I was quite clear with her about the danger of the situation. She is well and asymptomatic at the moment but without appropriate therapy will certainly die of lymphoma. At the same time there is no guarantee of success now that she has relapsed disease.

"No guarantee of success." Those were numbing words to me, but I still refused further chemotherapy treatment. I left his office and went to see the radiologist, Dr. Meredith. I left her office feeling uplifted. I can't explain it, but to everyone's surprise – including mine – I agreed to radiotherapy after the visit. We traveled back to Birmingham on April 16, 2008, for the follow-up from the diagnosis of relapsed T-cell lymphoma. My doctor wrote:

Restaging CT scans of the neck, chest, abdomen, and pelvis are actually negative and she does not have any measurable disease in the cervical area and the chest, abdomen, and pelvis were also negative. The PET scan from today shows a hypermetabolic right level II lymph node with an SUV of 3.6, and left level II lymph node with an SUV of 3.8, as well as increased FDG activity in the anterior mediastinum, probably related to brown fat. There are no other sites of disease. These were considered suspicious for involvement by lymphoma, although not clearly changed from 01/16/08. … I was quite clear with Ms. Wimes that this is not optimal therapy, and that she really ought to have systemic therapy followed by radiation but she is unwilling to consider chemotherapy. On that basis, I think that radiation is better than no treatment, as there is a chance (albeit lower) of a curable complete remission of this approach. Because this is contralateral to her original site of disease and she did not receive optimal therapy the first time around, despite the fact that she has not had a frank relapse in the left side, I agree with treating the neck bilaterally. She will proceed with radiotherapy; I will see her back about three months after she finishes that for reevaluation including CT scans…. Ms. Wimes understands that the odds of long-term disease-free survival are almost certainly lower with radiation than with chemotherapy.

I had radiotherapy treatments Monday through Friday for four weeks beginning April 21, 2008. I completed them on May 16, 2008. This was a breeze compared to the chemotherapy. I shouted, "Hallelujah!" on the last day and everyone heard it. They thought something was wrong and ran into my room. What no one knew was that I was surprised and excited that I actually completed the treatment.

I continued quarterly visits for about two years and then every six months. My doctor wrote on July 19, 2009, "Ms. Linda Wimes remains in remission now, 2 years after involving field radiotherapy for a local recurrence of CD20 positive ALCL (ALK-1 negative). While there is an ongoing risk of recurrence, I am delighted with her progress as she is." More visits followed from 2009 until 2013. The last report read: "Ms. Linda Wimes remains in clinical and radiographic remission…"

I am still staying in the Word of God and saying what it says. I continue to not be moved by what I hear and I continue to walk in the truth that "Jesus healed them all."

INTRODUCTION

"It's not good news. It's CANCER," the doctor said.

These words were delivered as I sat in his office on September 4, 2007. "It's cancer." How could this be? Only high blood pressure and arthritis were in my family line. And now – cancer?

My routine life of spending time with family, going to work and church, prison ministry, and serving others was being invaded. We were right in the middle of HIS Prison Ministries' Christmas for Inmate Children and the party was less than three months away. And now an uninvited guest – cancer – wants to visit. No invitation. It just showed up. I found myself in untraveled and foreign land, like the Israelites (Exodus 14:3).

Unlike Jed Clampett on the Beverly Hillbillies, I wasn't "shooting for food and up through the ground came a bubbling crude." No, that's not my story.

Life happens and sometimes it comes at us so hard and unexpectedly that everything looks bleak and dead. Like a barren land, we aren't sure which way to go or what to do. We wonder how much more we can take. We're not sure how or if we're going to make it. And if that is where you are, let me offer you hope. My circumstances were constantly changing, but I discovered some things that became more real to me as I journeyed down this road. These lessons for me are the structure of this book:

We all have an appointment with death.
Only God knows the date and time.

Believe in God, seek Him, and pray.

Get in the Word of God and find out what it says about your situation.

Understand God's power and authority.

Stick with the Truth (God's Word).

Facts are subject to change.

Truth remains the same to eternity.

Don't Limit God.

Have a supporting team.

Obtain peace and walk in it.

Stand, stand, stand.

Who is this crazy lady on this roller coaster ride you may ask? I am an ordinary person who dared to trust an extraordinary God. I have no medical background. I am not a Bible scholar and I don't know the Bible inside and out. Writing a book was not on my life's agenda, but it was on His. He knew it the whole time. It was a heavenly set-up. I now realize why I kept all of my medical records and have documented my journey from day one. What do I know about writing a book? Absolutely nothing! But I committed to being obedient and pushed myself to not leave 2019 – five years after starting to write – without completing it. It was delivered, like having a baby, on December 30, 2019.

The Lord knew that other lives could benefit, be touched, or even changed by sharing my testimony of what He has done in my life. After editing, editing, and editing, I am honored to share my story.

God is no respecter of persons[1]. He healed me and He can do it for you. I have to tell you one thing, though. You will have to be willing to die, physically and to yourself (your thinking) and rely on His leading. There may be times when these deaths

---

[1] Acts 10:34

are staring you right in the face. You just keep trusting and walking.

As you travel through this book, you will find lots and lots of scriptures. They were – and continue to be – my lifeline and a constant reminder of who God is and what I believe. You will find sections called a "Pause Break." Take the time and ponder what has been said.

Seek the Lord for whatever you may need. No situation is too hard for Him. Don't give in and don't you dare give up. Even in the most seemingly difficult situation, always remember that there is a God who loves and wants only the best for you. Don't look at your circumstances but rather to Him. He, alone, has the final word in our lives.

And another thing: if it seems at any time that something is repetitive, it's no typo; I repeated what I wrote. Some people get it the first time, but then there are those – like me –who take several times of hearing or reading something over and over again before it sinks in and sticks.

This book is my journey as I traveled: trusting God and not being moved by what I heard. This test has become my testimony and I gladly share it to encourage others to trust Him. Your test may be different. But know there is a God who can handle any test. He loves us unconditionally. He only asks that we trust Him.

I know lives are going to be changed. I'm one of those lives who is already experiencing the change.

All glory and honor belong to Him.

WILLING TO DIE
"A person's days are determined ..." Job 14:5

W hat a way to start a book – talking about Death. But the title of the book is, "You Have to Be Willing to Die." Even as I write, death is looming in the form of a coronavirus pandemic called COVID-19. It has turned our world upside down. The USA had 6,431,152 people infected and 192,818 deaths, with numbers consistently changing. Vaccines are under study. We practice social distancing, frequently wash hands with soap and water, and avoid touching our eyes, nose, or mouth at all costs. What we call "normal" no longer exists. Death is hovering like a vulture looking for its next meal.

It's understandable that we're afraid. Death sounds like a dark, unknown valley. It causes discomfort. I've lost four acquaintances within the last week.

After hearing I was diagnosed with cancer in 2007, I didn't know whether I would live or die during my journey. The Lord didn't tell me and I didn't ask. All I know is this: He said, "Do not to be moved by what you hear." I didn't ask for any other answers but I later wrote my obituary just in case death came:

"She leaves to cherish her memories: Her husband, "my man" as she calls him: Fred; two daughters: Shalunda and Christi; her middle child as she called her: Wendy Davis; grandchildren: Joshua, Donovan, Cameron; mother: Lucille Harrison; father, Charlie Harrison; siblings: Delores Harrison, Janice Ardis, Phillip Harrison; my friends Elaine, Sophia, Mary Jean, Big Momma/Daddy (Ida/Nate Smith), and the other Linda (Linda Smith Harrison); and a host of nieces, nephews and other relatives."

Sometimes, I would read the obituary section just to make sure my name wasn't listed. Although I didn't see it, I was told there were a couple of times it was reported that I was dead!

"Someone called and said you were dead!" my neighbor hollered as I headed to my car.

"Are you serious?" I asked, with a shocked look on my face.

"I told them if you were dead then I just saw a dead woman walking," he said.

The news spread to other family members. Some contacted the local hospitals. My niece, Jessica, telephoned and was uncontrollably crying. I can still hear between her sobs: "Auntie, Auntie, they said you were dead. They said you were dead."

I responded several times, "Jessica, Jessica, I can't be dead. Baby, you're talking to me."

My friend, Marvin, telephoned, "Linda, somebody called asking if you were dead. I told them I didn't think so. I had to call you for myself." Imagine a dead woman answering the phone.

Another time, Fred received several calls. "We're sorry to hear about Linda. You have our condolences." He never told me about the calls until I mentioned that some people were saying I was dead. That's Fred. Not much bothers him. Or maybe it didn't matter because he knew I was alive. It tickled him but not me. I wasn't dead! Several more people approached me saying, "I saw your name in the newspaper." I called the funeral home to see how this erroneous information was presented to the public. Their response: "We've been getting calls too from people thinking it is you."

I had never been in a situation like the one I was in. I called my daughters to make them aware that the news of my supposed death was spreading. I didn't want them to receive any condolence calls. It really could have been my time and I could have died because of the diagnosis, so the rumors felt very real. I knew where I would end up eternally, so that wasn't the issue. Death is inevitable, but it's still one of the hardest things to accept.

I aimed to find comfort in the blessings of life God had already given me just in case it was my time to die. The Lord had already given me a good life before the diagnosis. I already had a husband who loved me, had seen my daughters to maturity, and had a bonus of three grandchildren. I enjoyed my friendships and serving my community. What more could I have asked? I continued to walk in what God had spoken and left (and continue to leave) the decision of my living or dying up to Him.

Still, not many people sit around the table having casual conversations about dying. The mention of death changes the atmosphere. It tends to bring a spirit of gloom and doom. Who wants to hear, "I'm sorry but we've done all we can and you only have three to six months to live"? I didn't. I wanted to live! I didn't even like the thought of, "It's cancer." It had the sound and the "look" of death in it. Those I knew who experienced the diagnosis looked like they were already dead.

We tend to wait until death happens before we're forced to talk about it. My Daddy, for example, never liked talking about death. Like a virus, he always tried to avoid it. He would say, "It doesn't matter, just throw me in a pine box," or "I don't care what happens, I will be dead anyway." When Daddy died, he didn't have any insurance and you can probably figure out the rest of the story. (Please don't do this to those you love.)

My mom, on the other hand, taught us at an early age to prepare for death. She said, "A little piece of insurance is better than none at all." And she was right.

The blessing for me in the cancer diagnosis was that I gained a better grasp on the reality of death and on life in general. Facing death from a closer perspective than I had before, brought some scriptures to mind to settle my thoughts:

Show me, Lord, my life's end and the number of my days; let me know how fleeting my life is. You have made my days a mere handbreadth; the span of my years is as nothing before you. Everyone is but a breath, even those who seem secure.
Psalm 39:4-5

As disturbing and unpleasant as it may be, death is a part of life. Whether we like it or not makes no difference. It's a reality. These bodies of ours, made of dust, will return to the earth and our spirits to God (Ecclesiastes 12:7). The day is coming when the reports of your or my death will be true. Physical death is coming one way or the other, by death or His return. Only God knows the day, time, and hour.

Job 14:5 says, "A person's days are determined; you have decreed the number of his months and have set limits he cannot exceed." Hebrews 9:27 (KJV) says, "And as it is appointed unto men once to die, but after this the judgment."

For the believer, death is not the end but rather the beginning of a new existence with God. It is the door through which we must pass to gain entrance into the place He has prepared for us. He's coming back with the believers who have already joined Him for the believers who are still on earth[4]. Hallelujah! Thank you, Jesus!

Because we know that death is on its way, we need to prepare.

A DIFFERENT KIND OF DEATH

As we serve God's purpose, there is another death we must experience in addition to a physical death. It's called "dying to self." This death happens while we still have breath in our bodies. In this death, we die to self and anything contrary to the Word of God. We don't allow anyone or anything to elevate itself above God. "Anyone" includes ourselves and "anything" includes our perceptions, wrong thinking, and traditions. This is what the Pharisees and the teachers of the law in Jesus' day did. They revoked, rejected, set aside, and invalidated the word of God by hanging on to their traditions (Mark 7:13). Among the consequences for doing so are empty, hopeless lives.

---

[4] Hebrews 9:28

How do we die to ourselves? We yield to Jesus, let everything else go, and develop an intimate relationship with Him. We submerge ourselves like a submarine – emerging empty, and ready to be filled with nothing but the Word. Then, as His sheep, we will hear His voice and only follow Him[5].

As we continue to die to ourselves, we live a life pleasing to Him and impact the lives of others as we move forward on our journey of faith. Our journey of faith is like a kernel of wheat that travels once it is planted. John 12:24 says, "Very truly I tell you, unless a kernel of wheat falls to the ground and dies, it remains only a single seed. But if it dies, it produces many seeds."

Jesus gave us the example. He came. He was about His Father's business. He impacted those around Him. He gave His life for us on the cross. He declared, "It is finished[6]." And it didn't stop there. He arose with all power in His hands[7]. I am about to shout in here! His death and resurrection is why we are alive today.

If we truly believe that our existence is a result of His sacrifice, then we can also believe that His sacrifice includes our healing. Hear this: no matter the diagnosis, you are already healed. It's already done. The price has been paid:

But he was pierced for our transgressions, he was crushed for our iniquities; the punishment that brought us peace was on him, and by his wounds we are healed.
Isaiah 53:5

To experience this healing, we have to die to ourselves. The physical time of death is designated and we may experience physical healing many times before then, but the ultimate healing is in dying to ourselves and surrendering to Jesus. When this happens, the life we experience is the full life we were put here for in the first place.

---

[5] John 10:27
[6] John 19:30
[7] Matthew 28:18

Jesus is no stranger to bringing life when we believe Him. He raised the widow's son in the village of Nain (Luke 7:15). He raised the 12-year-old daughter of Jairus, a ruler of the synagogue (Mark 5:42). He raised Lazarus, the brother of Mary and Martha in Bethany, after he had been dead four days (John 11:44). And He raised Himself from the dead after he had been crucified (John 10:18). Jesus bore our sins in his body on the cross so that we might die to sin and live for righteousness; "by his wounds we are healed" (Isaiah 53:5).

Jesus was punished. He was whipped. Why? So, we could be made whole. Was the punishment He received because of our sins for nothing? I say not. So, until He calls us home at our appointed time, let's continue to die to ourselves and anything contrary to the Word of God.

You see, to live, we must die. If there is no death, then there is no resurrection to life. We no longer have to have a spirit of doom and gloom. We will live if we die. Death does not have the last word. Jesus conquered the grave. He overcame the power of death and opened everlasting life for all who believe. He has the final word.

...Then the saying will come true: Death swallowed by triumphant Life! Who got the last word, oh, Death? Oh, Death, who's afraid of you now?
1 Corinthians 15:54-55 MSG

Jesus said to Martha, "I am the resurrection and the life. The one who believes in me will live, even though they die; and whoever lives by believing in me will never die" (John 11:25-26). The scripture also says, "...Blessed are the dead who die in the Lord" (Revelation 14:13).

Romans 14:8 reminds us, "If we live, we live for the Lord; and if we die, we die for the Lord. So, whether we live or die, we belong to the Lord." We also have Philippians 3:20-21 MSG: *But there's far more to life for us. We're citizens of high heaven! We're waiting the arrival of the Savior, the Master, Jesus Christ, who will transform our earthy bodies into glorious bodies like his own. He'll make us beautiful and whole with the same powerful skill by which he is putting everything as it should be, under and around him.*

Pause Break – Pause Break!

It is appointed for man to die once, and after that comes judgment (Hebrews 9:27). Would you be ready to meet Jesus if your appointment was right now? Is it your desire that your life has an impact to leave a legacy that produces a productive harvest in the lives of others? This is a matter of eternal life or death. If you aren't ready, then I ask that you invite Jesus to come into your life as Savior and Lord. Accept Him and receive eternal life.

Your life will never be the same once you have made a conscious decision to accept Jesus as your Lord and Savior. Don't wait; tomorrow is not promised. *Forget tomorrow.* Our next breath isn't promised. Do it now.

I had the privilege and honor of leading my Daddy to the Lord, as the doctors had done all they could. He died less than 12 hours later as a redeemed child of God. What are you waiting for? Come on. It's your time to receive Him if you have not.

Here is a prayer you can say, but remember that your decision has to be made within your heart: *Dear Jesus, I thank you for loving me and choosing me even when I didn't choose you. I repent of my sins, for doubting you, and for living life as if I didn't need you. I ask you now to come into my heart. Save me. I'm willing to die to myself so that I may live in You. In your name I pray, Amen.*

I believe that if you made the decision to follow Jesus, then you are now on the path to heaven. You're saved. Welcome to the family of believers! Your healing – whether spiritual or physical – is on its best track in Jesus.

THE FACT OF THE MATTER

If we don't die to Christ spiritually, we'll physically die a lot quicker. Physical death may be looming but we don't have to be afraid when we've died spiritually because our Good Shepherd is with us. Psalm 23:4 reminds us:

Even when the way goes through Death Valley, I'm not afraid when you walk at my side. Your trusty shepherd's crook makes me feel secure. (MSG)

Even though I walk through the [sunless] valley of the shadow of death, I fear no evil, for You are with me; Your rod [to protect] and Your staff [to guide], they comfort and console me. (AMP)

Death is real and it happens. It doesn't have the last word. And it isn't the end of our story. A new day is coming. Revelation 21:1-4 says:

Then I saw "a new heaven and a new earth," for the first heaven and the first earth had passed away, and there was no longer any sea. I saw the Holy City, the new Jerusalem, coming down out of heaven from God, prepared as a bride beautifully dressed for her husband. And I heard a loud voice from the throne saying, "Look! God's dwelling place is now among the people, and he will dwell with them. They will be his people, and God himself will be with them and be their God. 'He will wipe every tear from their eyes. There will be no more death or mourning or crying or pain, for the old order of things has passed away."

And guess what else? When we physically die, we get a new resurrected body[8]. So, until that time, let's continue as King David and serve God's purpose in our generation (Acts 13:36).

When we are afraid, we can trust God. He is with us as we

---

[8] 2 Corinthians 5:1

walk through the *shadow* of Death. It looks like death, but it's not. It's a shadow.

Our Good Shepherd watches over us. We can walk in His peace despite the reports we've been given and in times of uncertainty. He is on our side and He is for us. Our hope is in the Lord. Our lives are in His hands. We continue to trust Him and His faithfulness.

Goodbye, Death. Your day is coming and you will be no more. But until then, we will trust, rest, and look forward to His return. We will not walk around as those without any hope. Our Redeemer lives and we win.

Okay, we made it through the Death chapter. We've had our talk. Now, let's move on.

-----------------2-----------------

WILLING TO EXPERIENCE GOD'S EXISTENCE AND REWARDS

"...anyone who comes to him must believe that he exists and that he rewards those who earnestly seek him." Hebrews 11:6

A Gallup poll was conducted in 2017 to gauge the number of respondents who believed in God[9]. The highest level of belief (87%) came when the questions required a simple "yes" or "no" answer. Belief dropped to 79% when respondents were given three options, one being whether "God" is something they believed in. The rest of the respondents were either not sure whether they believed in God or firmly said they did not believe in God.

A question, "Do You Believe in God or Not?" was also asked by Pew Research Center[10]. One-third of Americans responded they "do not" believe in the God of the Bible, but that they do believe there is some other higher power or spiritual force in the universe. About half of the respondents said they do not believe in a higher power or spiritual force of any kind.

The responses in the two surveys are probably not far from today's society. Some may be reluctant in believing in a God they cannot see. They're skeptical like Thomas when the other disciples told him they had seen the Lord. Thomas said, "Unless I see the nail marks in his hands and put my finger where the nails were, and put my hand into his side, I will not believe."

Jesus came a week later. He said to Thomas, "Put your

---

[9] Gallup Poll: How many Americans Believe in God? 2019
[10] Pew Research Center. When Americans say they Believe in God, What Do They Mean? 2018

finger here; see my hands. Reach out your hand and put it into my side. Stop doubting and believe." Thomas said to him, "My Lord and my God!" Then Jesus told him, "Because you have seen me, you have believed; blessed are those who have not seen and yet have believed" (John 20:25-29).

God will never cease to exist. He has no beginning or end. The Psalmist said:

In the beginning you laid the foundations of the earth, and the heavens are the work of your hands. They will perish, but you remain; they will all wear out like a garment. Like clothing you will change them and they will be discarded. But you remain the same, and your years will never end.
Psalm 102:25-27

We experience the realness of God as we look to Jesus. Philip said, "Lord, show us the Father and that will be enough for us." Jesus answered: "Don't you know me, Philip, even after I have been among you such a long time? Anyone who has seen me has seen the Father. How can you say, 'Show us the Father'?" (John 14:8-9). God is real. He was in the beginning and created the heavens and earth. Get to know (develop a relationship, spend time with) Jesus.

We have to settle our belief in God's existence and rewards if we desire to receive anything from Him. Although we can't perceive invisible things with our senses, we can judge them. We don't see the wind but we see the effects of it. We don't see the air but we breathe. Our belief is all by faith.

THE GREAT REVEAL

Existence is the state of being alive or being real. "Real" is described as actually existing as a thing or occurring in fact; not imagined or supposed, not imitation or artificial; genuine. As children, we believed Jesus existed because family, the preacher, and others said it or at least gave that impression.

They even talked like He was a real person and sometimes right in the room. We just followed their belief until there came a day we got the picture and acted just like the other believers did. We had an up-close and personal encounter. He became real. John 1:18 says, "No one has ever seen God, but the one and only Son, who is himself God and is in closest relationship with the Father, has made him known."

God reveals Himself in many ways. Hebrews 1:1-2 says, "In the past God spoke to our ancestors through the prophets at many times and in various ways, but in these last days he has spoken to us by his Son, whom he appointed heir of all things, and through whom also he made the universe." One way God reveals Himself is through the Scriptures. Second Peter 1:20-21 (AMP) says, "But understand this first of all, that no prophecy of Scripture is a matter of or comes from one's own [personal or special] interpretation, for no prophecy was ever made by an act of human will, but men moved by the Holy Spirit spoke from God."

God also reveals Himself to us through events. He allows events to occur in our lives to direct us, change us, and help us grow spiritually. He has a purpose for our life – to seek Him, reach out for Him, and find Him. We will find Him when we search for Him with all our hearts[11]. Psalm 19:1-2 says, "The heavens declare the glory of God; the skies proclaim the work of his hands. Day after day they pour forth speech; night after night they reveal knowledge."

Regardless of the way God chooses to reveal Himself or speak to us, He will never contradict His Word, and it will always bring glory to Him. Let's take Jacob, for example: "There he built an altar, and he called the place El Bethel, because it was there that God revealed himself to him..." (Genesis 35:7). I know God is real. I sought. I reached out. I found Him. I told Him about my situation. I waited to hear from Him. He told me the diagnosis before the doctors uttered the words "cancer, non-Hodgkin's lymphoma." He knew this

---

[11] Jeremiah 29:13

would be a journey I'd never traveled. He knew every word that would be spoken before it was said or I would hear them. He knew I needed to be told, "Don't be moved by what you hear."

Some of us may still need to be convinced that God is real. If we took the time to think about it, we would realize that somebody has been watching out for us. It wasn't happenstance. It was our loving God watching over his creation. He was there all the time. Yet, we didn't recognize Him. Think about the time you were almost in an accident or almost lost your life. What about the time you got the job you wanted? For some, it was the time you thought your childhood sweetheart was to be your spouse, but now you're shouting, "OMG, thank you, Lord!" That might ring the bell to the fact there's a higher power helping you make decisions. See, our real God is at work. God, who holds your very breath in His hands, allowed you to see this day.

Look around. Romans 1:20 (AMP) says, "For ever since the creation of the world His invisible attributes, His eternal power and divine nature, have been clearly seen, being understood through His workmanship [all His creation, the wonderful things that He has made], so that they [who fail to believe and trust in Him] are without excuse and without defense."

God is our Creator. Acts 17:26-27 says, "From one man he made all the nations, that they should inhabit the whole earth; and he marked out their appointed times in history and the boundaries of their lands. God did this so that they would seek him and perhaps reach out for him and find him, though he is not far from any one of us." The apostle Paul is a great example of someone whom God was not far from. Now, Paul wasn't always on the right (God) side. He was born Saul and was one of the bad boys persecuting Jesus' followers, but he had a "great reveal" of God as he neared Damascus on his journey. When a light from heaven flashed around him, he fell to the ground and heard a voice say to him, "Saul, Saul, why do you persecute me?"

"Who are you, Lord?" Saul asked. "I am Jesus, whom you are persecuting," he replied.
Acts 9:3-5

You see how Saul responded, "Who are You, Lord?" How do you call someone Lord if you don't even believe He exists? What would you have said if you heard a voice calling your name and asking, "Why are you persecuting me?" Would it get your attention? It did Saul and resulted in him having an up-close and personal encounter. God became real to him on that day. We now know Saul as Paul, one of the greatest apostles in the Bible.

Paul took the opportunity to share God's existence with those in Athens. While there, he noticed all of the idols, even one inscribed: "To An Unknown God." Paul stood in their meeting and told them about God. Some believed and had an up-close and personal encounter. God became real to them and He received the glory (Acts 17:23-31).

Later, in his suffering, Paul wrote: "…for I know Him [and I am personally acquainted with Him] whom I have believed [with absolute trust and confidence in Him and in the truth of His deity], and I am persuaded [beyond any doubt] that He is able to guard that which I have entrusted to Him until that day [when I stand before Him]" (2 Timothy 1:12 AMP).

Do you think God has changed? Do you think He is moved from His position of wanting to reveal Himself to us? If He hasn't moved from His position, but we feel He isn't there, then who has moved? We have.

HE STILL SPEAKS TODAY

In the same way God revealed Himself in many ways, the Bible records God speaking to people many times. He spoke to Moses to give instruction to the Israelites (Exodus 20:1). He spoke to Ezekiel the Prophet (Ezekiel 1:3). He spoke to Adam and Eve in the Garden (Genesis 2:16–17). And He still speaks today.

I've had many times where I didn't know what to do and I needed to hear from Him. One of those times I said, "Lord, I don't know what to do. If I do this, it will turn out this way and if I don't it could cause further harm." The Lord answered with a question. I responded and knew what I had to do. And I had a peace about it. Only a real God could have settled my troubled heart.

As smart as we may think we are, we need God's direction in our lives. We don't always know what to do, which road to take, or which move to make (it's like a maze). He knows we need Him, so He speaks to us in many different ways we will discuss later in the chapter. Don't be fooled by those who tell you that God doesn't speak today. Don't even argue with them. Leave the critics to themselves and their devices. This is your journey. Their journey is not yours. Because God hasn't revealed Himself or spoken to them doesn't mean He won't speak to you. You keep seeking and searching after Him.

For God does speak — now one way, now another — though no one perceives it. In a dream, in a vision of the night, when deep sleep falls on people as they slumber in their beds, ...
Job 33:14-16

A man with leprosy heard about and believed in Jesus. Leprosy was considered an incurable disease. Lepers were isolated and treated differently than other members of society. They were outcasts. Although he wasn't supposed to be there, the man came and knelt before Jesus. He said, "Lord, if you are willing, you can make me clean."

Jesus reached out his hand and touched the man. "'I am willing,' he said. 'Be clean!' Immediately he was cleansed of his leprosy" (Matthew 8:1-3). The man believed in the One whom God sent. Jesus was real to him. This man knew Jesus could make him clean if He was willing. Jesus is still willing.

Pause Break – Pause Break!

Maybe you haven't heard of Jesus or found your way to Him. He knows you, though. He knew you before you were born and even the name your parents would call you. Don't pull back. This book is for you as much as it is for the next person. I believe He purposed that you and I meet through these pages just to let you know how much He loves and cares for you. He sees and knows what's going on in your life right now. He wants you to get to know and trust Him. Find your way to Him. And keep on reading.

Jesus is the only way to God and the real truth and the real life. No one comes to God but through Him (John 14:6). We must believe (adhere to, trust in, rely on, and have faith) in Jesus (John 6:29). This relationship is real and personal. Faithful men started their quest to know God with the basic assumption that He made himself known, and not only in nature but in words. Elijah believed in God's existence. There was a time when he faced 450 prophets of Baal. They agreed on a plan: the god who answered with fire would prove to be, in fact, God. Baal prophets prayed all morning and past noon. Nothing happened — not so much as a whisper, not a flicker of response. Then came Elijah's turn. Elijah had the altar drenched and the trench filled with water. He prayed to God. God's power fell and burned the offering, the wood, the stones, the dirt, and even the water in the trench. The people saw it with their own eyes. Look at their response: "When all the people saw this, they fell prostrate and cried, "The Lord — he is God! The Lord — he is God!" (1 Kings 18:30-39).

TAKING GOD'S EXISTENCE SERIOUSLY

Even demons believe in God's existence. Are we not much better than them? They know God exists and that He has all power. James 2:19 says, "You believe that there is one God.

Good! Even the demons believe that—and shudder." There was an instance in the Bible where an unclean spirit asked, "What do you want with us, Jesus of Nazareth? Have you come to destroy us? I know who you are—the Holy One of God!" (Mark 1:24). Jesus rebuked the spirit, told him to be quiet and come out of the man the spirit possessed. And he came out. That spirit knew who Jesus was – the Holy One of God.

There were seven sons of Sceva – Jewish exorcists – who had no power or relationship with the Lord. They took it upon themselves to call on the name of the Lord Jesus over those who had evil spirits (Acts 19:13-16). The evil spirit said, "Jesus I know, and Paul I know, but who are you?" The spirit leaped on them and they fled out of the house naked and wounded.

We are made in God's image. He made us a little lower than the angels and crowned us with glory and honor (Psalm 8:5). We can't allow demons to have the upper hand on us in believing in His existence.

REWARDS FOR OUR BELIEF

The word "reward" denotes a return on something. The worker deserves his wages (1 Timothy 5:18). Great is your reward in heaven (Matthew 5:12). "For the Son of Man is going to come in his Father's glory with his angels, and then he will reward each person according to what they have done" (Matthew 16:27). We can find Him when we search for Him with all our heart (Jeremiah 29:13).

A person who diligently seeks after God will go to any length to find God and obey His Word. It's a life or death commitment. If a student has an exam and does not study, is he diligent? If a Christian says he loves his church but never supports the ministry, is he diligent?

Jesus said to his disciples, "Whoever wants to be my disciple must deny themselves and take up their cross and follow me. For whoever wants to save their life will lose it, but whoever loses their life for me will find it" (Matthew 16:24-25). Look at the reward in denying ourselves.

Caleb, at the ripe age of 85 years old, had no problem receiving his reward of the Promised Land. This reward was promised to him when he was 40 years old when he went on the mission with the other spies (Joshua 14:6-14). He wholly followed the Lord. King Abijah believed in the existence of God (2 Chronicles 13:8-18). He and his 400,000 men came against Jeroboam and his army of 800,000. Abijah said to Jeroboam:

And now you plan to resist the kingdom of the Lord, which is in the hands of David's descendants. You are indeed a vast army and have with you the golden calves that Jeroboam made to be your gods.
2 Chronicles 13:8

As for us, the Lord is our God, and we have not forsaken him. ...
2 Chronicles 13:10

God is with us; he is our leader. His priests with their trumpets will sound the battle cry against you. People of Israel, do not fight against the Lord, the God of your ancestors, for you will not succeed.
2 Chronicles 13:12

When we have a relationship with God, our heart's craving and our soul's longing will be to know more of Him. It's like a relationship where we're deeply in love with that special person. We hinge on every word that is said. We want to be in the person's presence all the time. We can't stop thinking about him or her.

If you're still not convinced that God exists, then tell me what god could foretell what would happen in the last days? Does this passage of scripture not describe the times we are living in right now?

But mark this: There will be terrible times in the last days. People will be lovers of themselves, lovers of money, boastful, proud, abusive, disobedient to their parents, ungrateful, unholy, without love, unforgiving, slanderous, without self-control, brutal, not lovers of the good, treacherous, rash, conceited, lovers of pleasure rather

than lovers of God – having a form of godliness but denying its power. …
2 Timothy 3:1-5

What god knows us (has our number) like our God?

You know when I sit and when I rise; you perceive my thoughts from afar. You discern my going out and my lying down; you are familiar with all my ways. Before a word is on my tongue you, Lord, know it completely.
Psalm 139:2-4

What god was in the beginning and created the heavens and the Earth? What god controls life and death? By God's grace, we believe in a God whom we cannot see. We rely on the eyes of faith until we get to see Him face-to-face. And He rewards those who believe in his existence and diligently seek Him.

There is no other god like our God. No other god could have given me peace and answered as He did during the cancer diagnosis. I am so grateful.

God has and will always exist. I rest my case!

Let's go after Him with our whole heart – the One true and Only God who exists and rewards.

----------------**3**----------------

WILLING TO ACKNOWLEDGE
GOD'S POWER AND AUTHORITY

"...Power belongs to you, God." Psalm 62:11

Power, Power, Power! Everywhere we turn, we hear about power. Everybody, regardless of their status, wants some. There are power structures in our homes, churches, schools, government, and streets: a standard for who is in charge, and who is next, and down the line. We have difficulty navigating our own lives sometimes, but we still want power.

Power is described as the ability to do something or act in a particular way. Authority is described as the power or right to give orders, make decisions, and enforce obedience. For instance, the flashing blue lights on a police car in our rearview mirror usually mean we should pull to the side. The officer is a legitimate source of authority and one with the right to pull us over. He or she has the power to issue a ticket if we fail to obey the traffic laws. However, the officer does not have the authority to make us do ten push-ups. Power and authority are limited.

There is only One who has all authority and power. His name is Jesus. All authority in heaven and on earth has been given to Him (Matthew 28:18). There are no limits to God's power or to what He is capable of doing, and there is absolutely nothing that can stop Him from achieving His desire.

God's power is confirmed through His Word from the beginning (Genesis) to the end (Revelation). With God, it is never a matter of whether He *can* do the things that we are asking Him. He can meet our needs, heal our diseases, and set us free. If we really understood God's power and authority, we would always seek Him first. We would run to Him like a runner heading toward the finish line.

When you search the Scriptures, you see God responding to those who had faith and understood His power and authority. I noticed that it made no difference about their status in life – saint or sinner. It never failed that when people called on Him, He answered.

The power and authority of God was evident when a Roman centurion asked Jesus for His help because his servant was ill in bed, paralyzed, and in terrible pain. Jesus offered to go to his house and heal him, but the officer responded, "Lord, I am not worthy to have You come under my roof, but only say the word, and my servant will be healed." The centurion understood authority and that all Jesus had to do was "say the word" for his servant to be healed. Jesus said He hadn't seen faith like that in all Israel. The centurion's servant was healed that very hour (Matthew 8:18 AMP).

Can you imagine the number of healings we would witness if we had an understanding of God's power and authority? It could make the headlines: "Jesus Says the Word and People Get Healed." This may sound unrealistic to some, but the truth is that it should be a reality to those who truly trust and believe in Him.

I love Western-themed movies with cowboys (*my age is showing*). I can take just about any incident and translate it into something about a cowboy. When I read about Elijah and King Ahab (1 Kings 18), I picture a showdown on Mount Carmel that resembles the scene in the old western movie, *Gunfight in Abilene*, when the situation between the farmers and the cattlemen intensifies. Grant Evers is murdered and Wayne has to strap on a weapon and settle things for himself and Abilene. In 1 Kings, Elijah straps on his weapon – the name of the Lord. The power of God shows up and everyone knows who has the power and acknowledges the Lord as God.

In the book of Daniel, three Hebrew boys – Shadrach, Meshach, and Abednego – were brought before King

Nebuchadnezzar for refusal to bow down and worship his golden image. This meant death. It sounds like the movie, *The Alamo: Thirteen Days to Glory,* where people were willing to die for what they believed. *I'm really telling my age.* Back to the boys and King Nebuchadnezzar.

"...King Nebuchadnezzar, we do not need to defend ourselves before you in this matter. If we are thrown into the blazing furnace, the God we serve is able to deliver us from it, and he will deliver us from Your Majesty's hand. But even if he does not, we want you to know, Your Majesty, that we will not serve your gods or worship the image of gold you have set up."
Daniel 3:16-18

One would think these boys were either crazy or brave. Who in their right mind would talk to the King in this manner? He had power and they were merely servants. They were bound and thrown into the fiery furnace. The King looked and was astounded because he saw four men, untied, walking around in the fire. He saw the boys weren't hurt and had them brought out. The King had a change of heart.

Then Nebuchadnezzar said, "Praise be to the God of Shadrach, Meshach, and Abednego, who has sent his angel and rescued his servants! They trusted in him and defied the king's command and were willing to give up their lives rather than serve or worship any god except their own God. Therefore I decree that the people of any nation or language who say anything against the God of Shadrach, Meshach and Abednego be cut into pieces and their houses be turned into piles of rubble, for no other god can save in this way." Then the king promoted Shadrach, Meshach, and Abednego in the province of Babylon.
Daniel 3:28-30

Now, the King knew who had all power and authority. He recognized that there was no other god that could deliver like this. He saw the results of the boys trusting their God. The boys were delivered, received a promotion, and God was glorified. Just like God was with the three boys, He will be with us. We must refuse to bow to anything that is not of Him. We are to take our stand and believe in His power and authority even if we lose our positions, friends, or our life. God is all-powerful and nothing is too hard for him. Jeremiah 32:17 says, "Ah, Sovereign Lord, you have made the heavens and the earth by your great power and outstretched arm. Nothing is too hard for you."

Pause Break – Pause Break!

Look around. Notice a sunrise or sunset. Have you ever stood on the beach and watched the points at high tide or the sea at low tide? That was God's power. He is the One who says the tides are going to come to this level, and no further.

Should you not fear me?" declares the Lord. "Should you not tremble in my presence? I made the sand a boundary for the sea, an everlasting barrier it cannot cross. The waves may roll, but they cannot prevail; they may roar, but they cannot cross it. Jeremiah 5:22

How do birds know to migrate? How do they know when and where to go? How do they keep going back to the same place time after time? God put the instinct within them when they were created.

Even the stork in the sky knows her appointed seasons, and the dove, the swift and the thrush observe the time of their migration. Jeremiah 8:7

God's power extends to the impossible, but it also extends to the very things that we are so familiar with and take for granted.

TAP INTO THE POWER

As I searched the scriptures during the cancer diagnosis, I noticed time and time again that many would run to God when something or someone concerned them. At times, the "someones" appeared to be "tell-tales", as we would say in my younger days. Tell-tales were always telling on someone or revealing others' secrets. In the case of the scriptures, we can classify some of the tell-tales as those who knew how to tap into God's power by running to Him to tell what was going on and to ask for help. King Asa in 2 Chronicles was a tell-tale. He told on Zerah. He and his 580,000 men went to war against Zerah and his one million men. Asa knew he couldn't win but he knew who could.

Then Asa called out to the LORD his God, saying, "O LORD, there is no one besides You to help in the battle between the powerful and the weak; so help us, O LORD our God, for we trust in and rely on You, and in Your name we have come against this multitude. O LORD, You are our God; let not man prevail against You." So the LORD struck the Ethiopians [with defeat] before Asa and Judah, and the Ethiopians fled.
2 Chronicles 14:11-12 AMP

Just like Asa, we get to choose whose power we will depend on. The enemy was defeated when Asa relied on the Lord, but not so when he relied on the king of Aram.

I know how it feels to rely solely on God. Fred and I wanted a second child, but I had a medical issue. The doctor said it was highly impossible to have another child. Well, that didn't stop us. We took the matter up with the Lord. We prayed and asked for another child before my 30th birthday. I walked around with expectations. I would place a setting at our table, saying out loud that "this is where our baby will sit." Sounds a little far-fetched, doesn't it? But it was my act of faith. I even saw our baby in a dream. I shared, "The Lord showed me that I was going to have a baby." One lady said, "I thought you were crazy." I was. I was crazy enough to believe in God. It would be ten years later before our prayer was fulfilled, but indeed, we had our second child before my 30th birthday. I call her our miracle baby. Who would have known that this child would be a member of my team when the visitor – lymphoma – arrived? No one knew but our all-knowing and all-powerful God, but we believed. Isn't that powerful?

In Genesis 17, God promised Abraham that he would be the father of many nations. First, he and his wife Sarah would have to have a seed (child). They were old; Abraham was 99 years old and Sarah was 89 years old. Sarah had never been able to have children. Still, God told them they were going to have a child and Abraham would be the father of many nations! God didn't take into account their age. Humanly speaking, this looked impossible and would take a miracle. Well, God fulfilled his promise. Abraham and Sarah got their son (Isaac) at the appointed time, just like He said.

If the Lord says something, believe Him. If He tells you that you will live and not die, take Him at His Word. The extent of your situation doesn't matter. No discussion or debate is needed. It matters not what anyone else says. Believe God!

How many times has the Lord given His Word concerning your circumstances? How many times have you responded with doubt? Why don't we just take Him at His word? Our situation may look dead, but we serve a God who has power over death and our circumstances. Does this not make you want to say, "I believe, help my unbelief"?

A little boy was out in the fields with his daddy. His daddy pointed to a huge rock and told him to pick it up. He went over and started to pull on it. He tried as hard as he could and he could not lift it.

"Try harder! Do anything you can to pick up that rock," said his daddy. This went on back and forth until the little boy finally said, "Daddy, I have tried everything I can and I just can't pick that rock up."

His daddy said, "You haven't tried everything yet."

The little boy said, "Oh yes, I have, Daddy."

The daddy said, "You haven't asked me to help you yet."

Many of us are just like this boy. We struggle and forget to ask our omnipotent God for help. Take heart; we're not the first and won't be the last.

While serving women who are incarcerated, I noticed that some had nowhere to go when they were released. There was nothing Fred or I could do because we had our own bills. We were preparing to send our youngest daughter, Christi, to college so our funds needed to be directed to her school. Well, the Lord took notice and began to deal with me about a particular abandoned house. It was run down to the run down. But He had a plan and worked it out. Others became involved and we obtained the house. He also provided everything that we needed to get the house up to code and standard. Never underestimate the power of God.

If you remember nothing else from this chapter, remember this: God's power is still the same as it was in the mightiest acts in scripture. His power does not change. It's everlasting. Unless we learn to trust and depend on Him, the power will do us no good.

POWER LIKE GOD'S

Not only is God's power available, but He has also given *us* the authority to use it. It's like a Power of Attorney. This authority is not based on *our* strength or power, but we have been granted the right to make decisions on His behalf.

When Jesus called the 12 disciples together, He gave them power and authority to drive out demons and to cure diseases. He sent them out to proclaim the kingdom of God and to heal the sick. They went from village to village, proclaiming the good news and healing people everywhere (Luke 9:1-6). After He was crucified, He told them to tarry in Jerusalem until they were endued with power from on high (Luke 24:49). They were to receive power when the Holy Spirit came upon them (Acts 1:8). Jesus said:

I assure you and most solemnly say to you, anyone who believes in Me [as Savior] will also do the things that I do; and he will do even greater things than these [in extent and outreach], because I am going to the Father. And I will do whatever you ask in My name as My representative], this I will do, so that the Father may be glorified and celebrated in the Son. If you ask Me anything in My name [as My representative], I will do it.
John 14:12-14 AMP

Do you see the Power of Attorney: "in His name" as "His representative?"

The word "ask" in the Greek means to demand or command. See how it works in this scripture: "And whatsoever you shall demand with commanding authority in my name that will I do that the Father may be glorified in the Son. If you shall command anything in my name, I will do it" (Matthew 21:21). We can speak to the mountain of our health and circumstances, tell it to be removed and cast into the sea and it will be done. It sounds like there are three steps: Speak – Tell it – And it will be done. God wants to show Himself strong on behalf of those whose hearts are loyal toward Him. He only needs someone to believe. Will you be that one?

Pause Break – Pause Break!

Jesus' death was for everyone, not a special few. There is nothing you or I can do to make Him not love us. You are just that special to Him. He is love. He wants us to believe Him for our deliverance, healing, finances, and whatever concerns us. We only have to believe and allow Him to work on our behalf. I'm tired of the mundane and just enough to get by. I want to see His power operating in my life to the fullest capacity. What about you? As much as we want it, He wants it more for us. Let's work on it.

God's power showed up recently at Mama Rosa's Pizza as my great-grands, Brooklyn, AJ, and I were eating. Our server returned to her area and suddenly fell to the floor. I heard the loud noise and immediately went to her side. No one else was in the building besides the cook, my two grands, the server, and me. She convulsed with seizures. I called the name, "Jesus." Who else could I call? A quote from Mother Teresa is, "You will never know God is all you need until He is all you have."

The convulsions continued and I kept calling, "Jesus." Two off-duty employees just happened to stop by and came to where we were. The seizures stopped. As her co-workers expressed thanks for me helping the young lady, I was able to witness to them about the name and power of Jesus. He was glorified. My two grands told their moms what happened. Both versions were different but both said, "Nana said Jesus, Jesus, Jesus." Even now, AJ will say, "Nana, Jesus, Jesus, Jesus" as she gets louder and louder. I am convinced that my grands will forever remember what happened that day when the name of Jesus was called.

There may be times we feel like Abraham and look at our circumstances rather than God's power. We might even want to offer God an alternative, or an "Ishmael" (Genesis 16). But know that the God we serve is who He says: "I am God Almighty." Even if the situation looks dead, remember Lazarus. God is always the same. He is everlasting.

Do you not know? Have you not heard? The Lord is the everlasting God, the Creator of the ends of the earth. He will not grow tired or weary, and his understanding no one can fathom. He gives strength to the weary and increases the power of the weak.
Isaiah 40:28-29

WALKING IN AUTHORITY

Say it with me: "God is our strength and our shield. When we are weak, He is strong. The name of the Lord is our strong tower. We can run to it and be saved. He is our defense and we don't have to be moved. Jesus, our Rock, is solid."

How quickly do we forget what He says when a storm comes and it looks like we may drown? A storm occurred on my journey in 2013. My original oncologist moved and I was assigned a new one. A CT of my abdomen revealed a suspicious lymph node, given a history of lymphoma. The doctor Impression and Plan stated:

Lymphoma. Note new lymph node in abdomen – this could be non-specific. She is asymptomatic at this point.... Discussed with her that if the lymph node increases in size, we may have to biopsy the masses to confirm suspicion but the question will be if she wants to proceed with chemotherapy or not. We do not need a decision at this time but this may be more relevant if we have unequivocal evidence of progression. ...

"It's not lymphoma," I said.

"Ms. Wimes, I am not saying it is lymphoma, but are you going to do chemotherapy if it is?" the doctor questioned.

"No, I am not doing any chemo," I replied.

The scans from the beginning indicated "no evidence of lymphoma in the abdomen." And now "new lymph node in abdomen – this could be non-specific." Something wasn't right. It was another roller coaster ride that I wasn't about to get on. All I could remember was not to be moved by what I heard.

I returned home and consulted a local specialist. Outpatient surgery was performed and there was no indication of cancer! You see, God wants to show Himself strong on our behalf. But we must settle two questions He asked:

Why Can't You Trust Me?
Is Anything Too Hard for the Lord?

We're talking about the same God who delivered the Israelites out of Egypt and allowed them to pass through the Red Sea unharmed and on dry land (Exodus 14:13-31). They lacked nothing on their journey. Their clothes and shoes didn't even wear out. They wanted meat and He gave them some. They needed water, and He provided that, too.

We have to make a decision. We can't be torn between two opinions. He's either our all-powerful God or not. Like playing a game of tennis, we have been served. The ball is in our court. Will we recognize His power and authority? Will we sit by and do nothing with it?

We have a choice to make. I choose to recognize and use His power and authority. What about you? Come on. Let's do this together and WIN.

4

WILLING TO ACCEPT THE WORD OF GOD

Jesus answered, "It is written: 'Man shall not live on bread alone, but on every word that comes from the mouth of God.'"
Matthew 4:4

God uses words. Whatever He said or called out in the Bible was made so. Check it out:

And God said, "Let there be light," and there was light. God saw that the light was good, and he separated the light from the darkness. God called the light "day," and the darkness he called "night. ..."
Genesis 1:3-5

In the stories within scripture, "God said" is always followed up by "It was So." God formed man from the dust of the ground and breathed into his nostrils the breath of life, and man became a living soul (Genesis 2:7). God said it and it was so! Our very creation was in God's hands because that's what He said.

Our life is in His hands. As an electrical appliance has to be plugged into a socket to operate, it is the same with us. We have to stay connected to God to live. We are a spirit with a soul living in a body. We need both physical and spiritual nutrition (food). If we don't get a healthy diet of both, we can become malnourished, which can lead to other serious problems.

Because He is our source of life, it only makes sense that His word – the Bible – is the food for our soul. It's as if the Bible is a grocery store that never closes, has no waiting line, and has aisles – the scriptures – that are always fully stocked.

No need for rainchecks. And guess what else? It's free. Come on, let's go shopping for some soul food.

HOPE WHEN WE NEED IT MOST

I am encouraged when I read the Word. It comes to life for me and I get excited (not that it takes much). I smile every time I think of how much He loves us. I'm smiling right now as I write. We are blessed! Psalm 1:1-3 (AMP) says:

Blessed [fortunate, prosperous, and favored by God] is the man who does not walk in the counsel of the wicked [following their advice and example], Nor stand in the path of sinners, Nor sit [down to rest] in the seat of scoffers (ridiculers). But his delight is in the law of the Lord, And on His law [His precepts and teachings] he [habitually] meditates day and night. And he will be like a tree firmly planted [and fed] by streams of water, Which yields its fruit in its season; Its leaf does not wither; And in whatever he does, he prospers [and comes to maturity].

Look at the benefits following the word "blessed." The person the psalmist is describing delights and habitually meditates day and night on God's precepts and teachings.

From the beginning until the end of my experience with cancer, my doctors wrote: "She was cheerful, she was alert and appropriate, remarkably calm, and appeared well." How can one be remarkably calm with a visitor called Cancer? Only by trusting, hoping, and taking God at His Word.

Everything we need can be found in the Word of God. God has given His Word as the source of hope. Romans 15:4 declares, "For everything that was written in the past was written to teach us, so that through the endurance taught in the Scriptures and the encouragement they provide we might have hope."

In the Word of God, we find promises made by our God, who keeps His covenant with his children. We can take God at His word because He doesn't lie. He does just what He says. Numbers 23:19 (KJV) says, "God is not a man, that he should lie; neither the son of man, that he should repent: hath he said, and shall he not do it? or hath he spoken, and shall he not make it good?"

God's track record is flawless (without blemish or imperfections; perfect). He always makes good on His promises. While it may seem like there are times that we don't get what we want when we want it, it's in these times that we must understand that God isn't slack to perform His Word. As a matter of fact, He hastens to perform His Word. He's just wanting us to believe and take Him at His word. Paul told Timothy, "All Scripture is God-breathed and is useful for teaching, rebuking, correcting and training in righteousness, so that the servant of God may be thoroughly equipped for every good work" (2 Timothy 3:16-17).

Isaiah 64:4 says, "Since ancient times no one has heard, no ear has perceived, no eye has seen any God besides you, who acts on behalf of those who wait for him." Isaiah 40:31 says, "but those who hope in the Lord will renew their strength…and not be faint."

GROUNDED WITH THE WORD OF GOD

How do we get to the place that we have hope in Him? By having an intimate relationship with Him. I pulled on that relationship when I first wrote my daughters about the diagnosis:

Shalunda and Christi: I will be having surgery on Wednesday am. The doctors aren't sure why the lump is still on my neck. They've tried to draw fluid and couldn't and the CAT Scan showed a lymph node. I saw the second doctor last week and will see the 3rd doctor on Tuesday. The second doctor agrees with the first about surgery. The 3rd doctor deals with head/neck tumor (he's a UAB graduate) and we'll see what he has to say. You all know I don't normally tell you all what is happening with me (medically) but this is a little different and I thought I would this time. I am confident though that the Lord is with me. That's the one assurance I have. Love, Mom.

I am in tears as I read this message I sent to my babies. The "ole" (not old) Linda couldn't have written this message. I had no relationship, hope, or confidence in the Lord. It's only as we spend quality time with Him that we have this intimacy. He will not force Himself on us. We get to decide how close we want the relationship to be. How do we get to know Him? By spending time in the Word. We can't just read it. We have to study, meditate, and do what it says.

The writer in Proverbs 3:3-4 (KJV) says, "Let not mercy and truth forsake thee: bind them about thy neck; write them upon the table of thine heart: So shalt thou find favour and good understanding in the sight of God and man." As we meditate on the Word of God, we are "writing these truths on the tablet of our heart." What is written on the tablet of our heart becomes the abundance of our heart from which our mouth speaks.

The Word never works for us by just sitting on a table or a shelf. It only collects dust. We must keep it before our eyes.

My son, pay attention to what I say; turn your ear to my words. Do not let them out of your sight, keep them within your heart; for they are life to those who find them and health to one's whole body. Proverbs 4:20-22

Did you notice "life to those who find them and health to one's whole body"? This is the remedy if we want life and health.

THE GAME PLAN

Jesus went through a time of testing in the wilderness (Matthew 4). He was without food for 40 days and 40 nights. During His fast, the devil came and challenged His identity as the Son of God. The devil told Him to command the stones to become bread. Jesus said, "…It is written: 'Man shall not live on bread alone, but on every word that comes from the mouth of God" (Matthew 4:4). There was no debate or argument but simply, "It is written." Jesus knew who He was. We can say the same when we know our identity. Doesn't this sound a lot like the "God said it" and "it was so" in the first section of this chapter?

Listen, the devil's mode of operation hasn't changed since the day he deceived Eve. He is cunning but his cover – to steal, kill, and destroy – has been pulled. He wants to take as many as he can into the eternal fire prepared for him and his angels. He's not that smart and he does not know it all. He only knows what we show him. So, the next time he comes around, give him the Word.

A coach and his team go over and over the plays for their games. They drill and drill. They practice and practice. We, too, are players on the field in a game called Life. We must keep the Word before our eyes, over and over again. Psalm 119:105 declares that the Word is a lamp to guide our feet and a light to our path. The Word we find is the Word we'll experience. Proverbs 7:1-3 (MSG) says, "Dear friend, do what I tell you; treasure my careful instructions. Do what I say and you'll live well. My teaching is as precious as your eyesight—guard it! Write it out on the back of your hands; etch it on the chambers of your heart."

Jesus said if we remain in Him and His words remain in us that we could ask whatever we wish and it will be done for us (John 15:7). Let's settle our hearts and do what He says.

CHOOSING HIS WORD OVER CIRCUMSTANCES

During the diagnosis, I found comfort and peace as I stayed in the Word. Again, I always responded, "All is well," when asked how I was doing. I chose not to say anything differently regardless of how I felt or looked. There certainly were times that my feelings and physical appearance did not look like what I was professing. There will be times when we feel overwhelmed, but remember that our feelings change like the number of hairs on our head or the cells in our body. The Word of God remains the same. We have to focus, get our eyes off our circumstances, go "shopping" in the Word, and claim the promises of God.

For no matter how many promises God has made, they are "Yes" in Christ. And so through him the "Amen" is spoken by us to the glory of God.
2 Corinthians 1:20

Now, focusing on God's word instead of the circumstances doesn't happen overnight. It's a process. So, keep pressing forward. If you get off track (unfocused), get back on. Even during my journey, there were other issues going on in my life. I made the decision that as much as my heart ached, I couldn't handle it all at the same time. My dwelling on the matters couldn't change the situations, so I kept focusing and refocusing on the Word of God. Staying in the Word helped me to handle the constant changes on my journey. It was like the Truth was on trial on the witness stand with a raised right hand saying, "So help me God." I stuck with the Word and the Truth never changed. Truth prevailed.

The Word of God is the final authority in our lives regardless of our circumstances. The Word of God is truth and is a higher form of facts. We know facts to be those things that are "known with certainty," but just because something is a fact or circumstance doesn't make it the Truth. Truth is *our* reality. As a child of God, the Word of God should be more real to us than our circumstances. We don't deny facts, but when they are contrary to God's Word, we can deny them the right to exist in our lives. The enemy will try to make us imagine something that does not exist to cause us to waver from the Truth. Fiction is produced by imagination and is not based on facts.

There was a woman with an issue of blood (Mark 5:25-34). It was a fact she suffered and endured 12 years of illness while in the care of many physicians. It was not a fact that her life would end that way, though. One day, this woman touched the hem of Jesus' robe and was healed by doing so. Her healing caught the attention of Jesus even in the midst of a large crowd. What was so different about her? What was her background?

Was she single, divorced, widowed, or fending for herself? We don't know, but what we do know is this statement of Truth: she heard about Jesus, pushed past her circumstances, settled what she believed and spoke it ("I shall be made well"), and touched the hem of His garment. Her bleeding stopped. She felt she was healed. She got what she declared.

Pause Break -- Pause Break!

The woman with the issue of blood caught Jesus' attention. And Jesus said her faith healed her. When is the last time you've caught His attention? Are we sitting around and allowing our circumstances to get the best of us? Are we willing to do whatever it takes to get to Him? Do we want to hear Him say, "Your faith has made you well?" Then, we have to get up from where we are, push past our circumstances, and start walking (in faith)! Come on – start walking.

Whatever we encounter in our lives may be a fact at the time but God's Word is the truth about us. We don't have to live our lives out of our circumstances, but rather out of the Truth and our relationship with Him.

Yes, Lymphoma invaded my body. I didn't give it an invitation. I could have died. Who could I turn to? I had never seen or been around anyone diagnosed with lymphoma. The ones I met with other cancers looked like they had been on the "rough-rough" side of the mountain. I wasn't hearing anyone say God had spoken to them or that they were walking by faith. Their conversation and concentration were about what the doctor was saying or their feelings. I get it, but my life was at stake and I needed help. I wasn't convinced I was going to get it from them. So, I searched the Word and discovered the real Truth. I found that Jesus was wounded for our transgressions and that we are healed and made whole. He took our infirmities and bore our sicknesses. He spoke and healed them.

I wasn't about to sit and do nothing. My life was on the line. Are you willing to do what it takes to get what you desire or will you continue to look at your circumstances? You get to decide. I needed healing, so I searched for scriptures about healing. It may be peace, finances, addictions, relationships, or something else for you. Go shopping and seek out those scriptures. Then, meditate and confess them over your life. Remember, focus on the Word—not your circumstances. We can stand on the Word of God because it is forever settled. Isaiah 40:8 says, "The grass withers and the flowers fall, but the word of our God endures forever." The Word of God is the truth about us in all areas of our lives.

What you say goes, God, and stays, as permanent as the heavens. Your truth never goes out of fashion; it's as up-to-date as the earth when the sun comes up. Your Word and truth are dependable as ever; that's what you ordered—you set the earth going. If your revelation hadn't delighted me so, I would have given up when the hard times came. But I'll never forget the advice you gave me; you saved my life with those wise words. Save me! I'm all yours. I look high and low for your words of wisdom. The wicked lie in ambush to destroy me, but I'm only concerned with your plans for me. I see the limits to everything human, but the horizons can't contain your commands! Psalm 119:89-96 MSG

You may be thinking, "Well the Word of God may be the truth but my circumstances aren't lining up." Remember, it's a process and your circumstances are subject to change. But the truth about you is whatever is written in the Word, and it will never change. Keep meditating and reminding yourself that Jesus is greater than your circumstances.

Focus and refocus. You've parked in what-ifs, misery, fear, depression, and torment long enough. Isn't it time to do something different? Get yourself in the Word and allow the Holy Spirit to speak to you by the truth of the Word of God.

MEDICINE FOR THE SOUL

When we go to the doctor and he or she prescribes medicine, the majority of us follow the instructions. So, why would we not follow the Great Physician's directions? Man-made prescriptions have side effects such as dizziness, cough, headache, diarrhea, fatigue, low blood pressure, and loss of appetite. The side effects of God's prescription are simple: Life. It's health to one's whole body. His direction is simple, too:

My son, pay attention to what I say, turn your ear to my words. Do not let them out of your sight, keep them within your heart; for they are life to those who find them and health to one's whole body. Above all else, guard your heart, for everything you do flows from it. Keep your mouth free of perversity; keep corrupt talk far from your lips.
Proverbs 4:20-24

Turning our ear to God's words is more than just putting our physical ears in a position to hear the Word. It also requires us to actively engage with God's Word so that we can believe and obey it.

Dear friend, listen well to my words; tune your ears to my voice. Keep my message in plain view at all times. Concentrate! Learn it by heart! Those who discover these words live, really live; body and soul, they're bursting with health.
Proverbs 4:20-22 MSG

Jesus said if we love Him, we will do what He says (John 14:23). Do we love Him? Then, let's take our medicine. Let's keep the Word before our eyes and not let it depart from our mouth[14]. Let's be "Word Poppers"! No such word, but it sounds like something we should do: pop the Word of God. Let's deposit the Word in our hearts and allow it to change us from

---

[14] Proverbs 4:21

the inside out. The Word is not like human medicine that treats symptoms. It gets to the root of it.

I've wished the doctor had gotten to the root of my issue in the beginning when it was a small abscess on my scalp behind my left ear. Just maybe the glands in my neck wouldn't have swollen. And just maybe I would not have journeyed down the cancer road. Nevertheless, the Great Physician got to the root of the problem. I took my medicine (the Word) and refused to be moved. I got to enjoy the side effects.

My doctor and I had several conversations about me stopping treatment. He was clear about his concern that I had not had enough therapy to be cured. He asked, "Ms. Wimes, are you going to do the chemo?"

After being asked three times I responded, "No, I am not doing any chemo! Dr. Foran, I believe healing starts from the inside. I'll take Jesus healed them all. I am willing to die for what I believe. You gave me no guarantee with the chemo. I've planned to see Jesus one day. I have nothing to lose."

I listened as he shared how he viewed healing and voiced disagreement with my decision. I wasn't trying to change the way he believed, nor was he about to change my stand. You see, I read the Word. I believed the Word of God as much as the doctor believed in his plan of treatment for me. I learned to take the Word of God and deposit it in my heart just like we deposit money in the bank. Then, I could make withdrawals whenever I wanted or needed to. And you can, too! Don't you love it? God's system (the Word) is always operational and is never down for maintenance. There's no limit to what He can do!

NO EXPLANATION NEEDED

We are to open our mouths and speak not words of sickness and disease, discouragement and despair, but words of life, faith, hope, and healing. We follow the last step of the prescription: we speak the Word of God and call ourselves healed in Jesus' name. We release words of faith out of our mouths. Again, my go-to words were always "all is well,"

WILLING TO ACCEPT THE WORD OF GOD 67

regardless of my circumstances. No explanation was necessary.

Let's go back to the woman with the issue of blood who touched Jesus. What was so different about her touch when so many people were in the crowd? She knew the Truth and she acted on the Truth rather than her circumstances. Now, nothing against women because I am one myself, but when we tell you the whole truth, you get the "whole truth so help me God." We will do our best to not miss a point. Imagine the woman with the issue of blood opting instead of touching Jesus to explain to Him: "I went to Dr. Aplin and he said it was a hemorrhoid. I took the medicine, but it didn't work. Then I went to Dr. Broom and he gave me a different medication. And that didn't work either. I went to several more doctors. Nothing has worked and I've gotten worse." Can you picture it?

Jesus said, "Whosoever shall say unto this mountain, Be thou removed, and be thou cast into the sea; and shall not doubt in his heart, but shall believe that those things which he saith shall come to pass; he shall have whatsoever he saith" (Mark 11:23 KJV). Notice the word "saith" appears three times while the word "believe" appears once. Did you also notice that He did not tell us to talk *about* the mountain? He told us to talk *to* it. Most of us talk about our circumstances rather than speak to them.

Our words are crucial. We have what we say. If only we realized that what we magnify grows. If we want different, we have to speak differently. It's time to say what we really want.

Some people say confession is good for the soul. Well, I have one to make. I have a hard time listening to people talk more about their circumstances than what God can do. I want so badly for others to know that God can help them. That's why I willingly share my testimony and encourage others to speak the Word (read more about testimonies in Chapter 10). If we desire to see a change, then we must say what He says. Let's be imitators of Jesus and say what God says. If you don't feel you have faith right now, stay in the Word until you get it. Remember, faith "cometh by hearing, and hearing by the word of God" (Romans 10:17 KJV). Jesus said:

... Pay attention to what you hear. By your own standard of measurement [that is, to the extent that you study spiritual truth and apply godly wisdom] it will be measured to you [and you will be given even greater ability to respond] – and more will be given to you besides.
Mark 4:24 AMP

Read, study, meditate, listen to tapes, and watch videos of faith-filled teaching until God's Word about whatever you're facing is more real to you than the circumstances or symptoms and more relevant than your need to explain.

Results may not always feel sudden. Do we stop taking the allergy medicine prescribed by our doctor if we don't stop sneezing right away? No! Don't get discouraged if you don't see immediate results. Take your spiritual medicine and keep following the prescription. Do your part and let God do His. He knows exactly what He's doing. He has been in practice since the beginning of time. And besides, He created us. Who knows more about creation than its maker? He even knows the number of hairs on our head[15].

AFTER YOU'VE DONE ALL YOU CAN

I am a living witness that the Word works. I've had and continue to have opportunities to experience it. Two hair bumps appeared on the right side of my neck in February 2008, which was about four months after I stopped the chemo treatments. I thought nothing of it because I've had them before. I just thought my hair was trying to come back since I lost it all due to the chemotherapy. My daughter, Shalunda, and I popped the bumps. One healed and the other had an issue. I

---

[15] Luke 12:7

saw a local dermatologist on February 28, 2008, who removed the hair from the spots. The bumps on my neck didn't appear to be improving. I went back to the dermatologist on March 6, 2008, and she performed a punch biopsy which showed an "abscess atypical infiltrate suggesting lymphoma". The pathology report indicated T-cell lymphoma with abscess.

The dermatologist telephoned and said, "Mrs. Wimes, it's cancer. Your cancer has come back."

"And how did you come up with something like that?" I asked. I thought, how could this be? There was never any involvement of the right side of my neck. The PET/CT scans report indicated involvement only in the left area of my neck.

My first thought was, "The chemo caused it because I read it could cause other cancers." I even asked my doctor if chemo could cause cancer but he never gave me a "yes" or "no" answer. He would always say, "Well, Ms. Wimes, it takes out the bad cells and it takes out some of the good ones too."

I asked again because he didn't really answer my question. He responded the same when I asked again and after the third time I said, "Okay."

I had just seen my oncologist on January 16, 2008, and felt well. The information from the dermatologist made it seem like the winds and waves were blowing again. I had gone down this road before but this time I was ready. I was already taking daily doses of my medicine (the Word). I remembered to not be moved by what I heard and I had on His armor (Ephesians 6:14-18). God had done it once and I figured He was about to show out again.

The dermatologist informed my doctor of the results and I was scheduled to see him the following Monday. My doctor called the Friday before the appointment. "Ms. Wimes, Ms. Wimes, they said the cancer came back."

"Ain't no cancer came back!" I responded.

"Are you going to allow me to treat you?" he asked.

"I am not doing any chemo!"

"Ms. Wimes, Ms. Wimes, what am I going to do?"

"I don't know," I replied, "but I am not doing chemo. I guess you'll have to come up with something."

He then asked me to tell him what was going on. I told him about the two hair bumps, that they were nothing and just the size of a small pea. We settled on me coming in on my regularly scheduled appointment on March 31, 2008, rather than the emergency appointment the nurse scheduled. I am so grateful that the Lord prepared me from the beginning. He knew what would be said and what I would hear.

When Fred and I made it to the appointment and the doctor asked how I was doing, I gave my same response that all was well. He asked me where the area was that the dermatologist was concerned with and I pointed to the area.

He said, "Ms. Wimes, I can't feel anything."

I gave him my crazy look and said, "I told you it wasn't nothing!"

Fred and I returned to the doctor about 15 days later. He reviewed the CT and PET scans and said, "Ms. Wimes, that was minor." Minor! Have you ever heard of cancer being called minor? Although he told us it was minor, I am not sure his clinical notes expressed what he said.

Ms. Wimes has an isolated localized relapse of lymphoma biopsy proven on punch biopsy .... I was quite clear with Ms. Wimes that this is not optimal therapy, and that she really ought to have systemic therapy followed by radiation but she is unwilling to consider chemotherapy. ... I will see her back about three months after she finishes radiotherapy. .... I feel like she really should be receiving systemic therapy and she has declined. I am in agreement with radiation with "curative intent." Ms. Wimes understands that the odds of long-term disease-free survival are almost certainly lower with radiation than with chemotherapy.

Fred and I returned about five months later. By that time, I had completed radiation treatment. The doctor's notes:

On examination, she was cheerful, she looked very well. ... She was very well. ...She is in clinical and radiographic remission. Ms. Wimes understands explicitly that this was not the optimal planned therapy for her disease as she abandoned systemic chemotherapy early on. Nevertheless, a minority of patients may be cured with radiotherapy for localized aggressive lymphoma even T-NHL, and therefore I am hopeful. Her chances are approximately 30% of long-term disease-free survival. She is in clinical and radiographic remission. A minority of patients may be cured with radiotherapy."

Here we go again with the facts changing. Yet, the truth remained the same. I was still standing on the Word. In spite of what the doctor said or wrote, I never took ownership of the facts in the case. I never called the visitor *my* cancer. I hadn't even invited it. I would always say, "They say." This may sound like I was in denial but I wasn't. I just knew the Truth. I read the scripture that said you have what you say. I wasn't about to claim or say the cancer was mine. Who in their right mind would want cancer? It made no difference in the number of times I heard the doctor say or write, "Ms. Wimes" and "cancer" in the same sentence. Nope, I took no ownership!

WORDS AND ATTITUDE

If you've been saying what they say, go and get yourself a Word alignment. You know, like a wheel alignment. Align yourself with the Word and start talking straight. What do you have to lose? If we understood the severity of our words, we would pay close attention to what comes out of our mouths.

When we say something out loud enough times, our words become the truth not only in our mind but in the minds of everyone hearing us. You may be surprised who's listening and watching. Even my mom paid attention to me during the diagnosis. She told me one day, "You never said the cancer was yours. You always said, 'They say'." One of my providers said, "Ms. Wimes we knew if anybody would make it that you would because you had attitude." And I sure did. This was my life and it was like God and I were in the same "Match of Life" with boxing gloves (although He didn't need any). I wasn't going down without a fight of faith. I trusted the Word of God and that was all to it.

Your attitude is very important in all circumstances. A survey was conducted among patients who were asked to classify their health as poor, fair, good, or very good. Those who chose "very good" were about 70% less likely to die within three years than those who answered "good." They had three times the survival rate of those who claimed "poor" health.

A study of more than 5,000 people over the age of 65 found that a poor image of one's health – regardless of other risk factors – roughly doubled the risk of death within five years. A pessimistic outlook proved to be deadlier than congestive heart failure or smoking 50 or more packs of cigarettes every year[16]. This information points to one suggestion: get yourself a good attitude and speak the Truth!

Our faith must be in the Word of God, which is the Truth, the whole truth, and nothing but the truth. God made that easy when He gave each of us the measure of faith[17]. It's ours. Use it and start speaking and acting like whatever "it" is has already been done.

Pause Break – Pause Break!

Do you want to be free? Jesus said, "… If you stick with this, living out what I tell you, you are my disciples for sure. Then you will experience for yourselves the truth, and the truth will free you" (John 8:31-32 MSG). We can rise above our circumstances and be set free by the Truth. Just as Jesus was speaking to the Jews who believed, He's speaking to you and me right now. We have to

---

[16] Healthday: Does Your Attitude Affect Your Health? 2020
[17] Romans 12:3

believe in Him and hold to his teachings. And the truth sets us free. Are we desperate and willing to do what it takes to be set free? Then let's get ourselves an attitude that won't be moved. As my daughter, Christi, says, "Stay right there."

Even when we feel hopeless, we have nothing to lose. Take God at His Word and do what He says. Ask Peter:

When He had finished speaking, He said to Simon [Peter], "Put out into the deep water and lower your nets for a catch [of fish]." Simon replied, "Master, we worked hard all night [to the point of exhaustion] and caught nothing [in our nets], but at Your word I will [do as you say and] lower the nets [again]." When they had done this, they caught a great number of fish, and their nets were [at the point of] breaking; so they signaled to their partners in the other boat to come and help them. And they came and filled both of the boats [with fish] … "
Luke 5:4-7 AMP

Remember to fellowship with God (John 15:4), spend time in His Word (Psalms 1:1-3), and hide it in your heart. It remains the same and it never changes. You can trust it. Hear and obey His voice (John 10:27). Wait on Him (Isaiah 40:31). And don't be moved.

WILLING TO PRAY

*"Rejoice always, pray continually, give thanks in all
circumstances; for this is God's will for you in Christ Jesus."*
1 Thessalonians 5:16-18

Prayer – to talk and listen to God – is something you have
probably been doing for longer than you thought. We did it
even if we didn't understand or know the significance. As a
child, many of us memorized Psalm 23:

The LORD is my shepherd, I lack nothing.
He makes me lie down in green pastures, he leads me beside quiet
waters, he refreshes my soul.
He guides me along the right paths for his name's sake.
Even though I walk through the darkest valley, I will fear no evil, for
you are with me; your rod and your staff, they comfort me.
You prepare a table before me in the presence of my enemies.
You anoint my head with oil; my cup overflows.
Surely your goodness and love will follow me all the days of my life,
and I will dwell in the house of the LORD forever.

We probably added in an "amen" at the end. Before bed, we
would probably say, "God bless Daddy, God bless Momma,
God bless grandmama and God, bless my dog, Homer. Amen."

Today, I get to hear my great-grands pray over their food
by chanting, "God is great. God is good. Let us thank Him for
our food. By his hands, we are fed. Thank you, Lord, for our
daily bread. Amen."

Most of us have experienced prayer in some form, but do
we understand its importance?

THE FACTS ON PRAYER

It has been said that the word "pray" is used 121 times in the Bible, not including the various conjugations of the verb. Then there's "prayed" at 68 times, "prayer" at 106 times, "prayers at 32 times, "praying" at 36 times, and "prays" at 12 times, for a total of 375 times[23].

Other passages contain the concept of prayer without using the word. Examples are Luke 10:2, where Jesus admonishes the disciples to ask God for workers to help in spreading the message of the cross, and James 1:5 (MSG), which says, "If you don't know what you're doing, pray to the Father. He loves to help…"

Prayer is simply communicating with God. We pray from our heart (soul) freely, spontaneously, and in our own words. Let me be the first to apologize if you've not prayed because others have made it seem so hard when it's not. Prayer is as necessary to the spiritual life as air is to the natural life, so my prayer is that this chapter will get you back into gear to start praying again. Prayer is just saying what's on your heart, taking the situation out of our hands and putting it in His hands. We're admitting that God is greater and knows what is best.

I prayed on my journey and God answered. I had no formula. I don't know if He saw the sincerity of my heart and extended grace or just knew I was looking to Him, but I do know that I was in a good place to be – looking to Him. His Word says in Psalm 19:14 (AMP), "Let the words of my mouth and the meditation of my heart Be acceptable and pleasing in Your sight, O Lord, my [firm, immovable] rock and my Redeemer." I was indeed redeemed.

Here's my disclaimer: I am not the guru on prayer. I don't have any formulas. I leave that up to the proclaimed prayer experts. I rely on the Holy Spirit to intercede for me (Romans

---

[23] NIV Exhaustive Concordance

8:26), and I look to Jesus as my example and leave the results to Him. I keep it simple. Everybody is different and there are many prayer books on the market. You'll have to find your comfort zone.

Wherever you are in your prayer life, I encourage you not to try to be like anyone else. Be *you*, the person who God made and is still working on. Just spend some time in prayer and get to know Him.

WHY WE PRAY

Talking to God through prayer is not a 21st-century movement. Praying is the manner by which our lives are renewed and our next steps are clarified. It has always been that way. This started long before you and I were born.

We can find from Genesis to Revelation where men began to call on the name of the Lord with the prayer, "Come, Lord Jesus." Moses asked the Israelites, "What other nation is so great as to have their gods near them the way the Lord our God is near us whenever we pray to Him?" (Deuteronomy 4:7). God spoke to Solomon, "If My people who are called by My name will humble themselves, and pray and seek My face, and turn from their wicked ways, ..." (2 Chronicles 7:14).

One of my favorite passages is 2 Chronicles 20 where the Moabites, Ammonites, and Meunites declared war against King Jehoshaphat. King Jehoshaphat didn't know what to do. Without hesitation, he stood in God's presence in the temple and prayed:

Lord, the God of our ancestors, are you not the God who is in heaven? You rule over all the kingdoms of the nations. Power and might are in your hand, and no one can withstand you. ... But now here are men from Ammon, Moab and Mount Seir, ... For we have no power to face this vast army that is attacking us. We do not know what to do, but our eyes are on you.
2 Chronicles 20:6-12

God answered and said:

Do not be afraid or discouraged because of this vast army. For the battle is not yours, but God's. Tomorrow march down against them. ... You will not have to fight this battle. Take up your positions; stand firm and see the deliverance the Lord will give you, Judah and Jerusalem. Do not be afraid; do not be discouraged. Go out to face them tomorrow, and the Lord will be with you.
2 Chronicles 20:15-17

Jehoshaphat and the people fell down in worship before the Lord. Then some Levites stood up and praised the Lord. They were very loud – not quiet at all. Can you imagine that happening in some of our churches?

We could almost model what Jehoshaphat did. The model would be a prayer to God, receiving the Word of the Lord, worshipping, going out in faith, singing, praising, and standing still as God fights – and wins – the battle. Let's do it and watch God fight and win our battles. We can do it when we've prayed, turned it over to Him, and have taken a position to stand. He did it for King Jehoshaphat and He will do it for us.

HOW TO PRAY

You may say, "I don't know how to pray or where to start." No problem. If prayer is an entirely new concept to you, I again want you to know that prayer is not hard. Do you have a trusted friend or a favorite pet? Surely, you have one. If not, think of someone or something of which you're fond. Then, talk to God just like you would talk to them or it. Are you still not feeling it? Say, "Lord, teach me how to pray." Now breathe, sit back, relax, and be quiet for a moment. Are you ready? If not, start over again and do it as many times as you need to. Then when you're ready, start the conversation and tell Him what is on your heart. Now stop, listen, and allow the Holy Spirit to help you pray. Open your mouth and speak from your heart. Pray God's Word. Look in the Bible. The Bible is full of prayers.

Romans 8:26-27 (AMP) says, "In the same way the Spirit [comes to us and] helps us in our weakness. We do not know what prayer to offer or how to offer it as we should, but the Spirit Himself [knows our need and at the right time] intercedes on our behalf with sighs and groanings too deep for words. And He who searches the hearts knows what the mind of the Spirit is, because the Spirit intercedes [before God] on behalf of God's people in accordance with God's will."

Here are a few things that I have come to realize about prayer as I read the Word:

There is no correct or certain posture for prayer. In the Bible people prayed on their knees (1 Kings 8:54), by bowing (Exodus 4:31), on their faces (2 Chronicles 20:18, Matthew 26:39), and while standing (1 Kings 8:22). You may pray with your eyes open or closed, quietly or out loud, in whatever way you are most comfortable and least distracted.

We are to pray continually. Read 1 Thessalonians 5:17. It does not matter where. Pray in private, public, in or out of bed, at Church, work, in the bathroom, on the toilet, in the shower, while driving, just wherever. It doesn't bother God.

We are to follow Jesus. Jesus was always praying and set the example for us. He prayed alone, before meals, before important decisions, before healing, after healing, and to do the Father's will. Jesus told his disciples a parable to show them that they should always pray and not give up (Luke 18:1). Prayer was His lifestyle.

One of Jesus' disciples observed him and said, "Lord, teach us to pray, just as John taught his disciples" (Luke 11:1). You've probably heard and said it yourself.

And he said unto them, When ye pray, say, Our Father which art in heaven, Hallowed be thy name. Thy kingdom come. Thy will be done, as in heaven, so in earth. Give us day by day our daily bread. And

forgive us our sins; for we also forgive every one that is indebted to us. And lead us not into temptation; but deliver us from evil.
Luke 11:2-4 KJV

Lord, help us to follow your example.

It does not matter how long you pray. Pray as long as it takes. Peter prayed three words, "Lord, save me!" (Matthew 14:30). There is no formula. No three cups of this or six teaspoons of that. Just talk to God, whether it's one, three, or ten words.

Don't compare yourself with others. We are unique individuals and communicate differently. Some of us are eloquent in speech and some of us, like me, are just plain and straight to the point. Pray in the spirit or pray in words you understand (1 Corinthians 14:15).

You can call on the elders. I read it in James 5:14-16:

Is anyone among you sick? Let them call the elders of the church to pray over them and anoint them with oil in the name of the Lord. And the prayer offered in faith will make the sick person well; the Lord will raise them up. If they have sinned, they will be forgiven. Therefore confess your sins to each other and pray for each other so that you may be healed. The prayer of a righteous person is powerful and effective.

I kept having a strong urge to be anointed and prayed over before we left to see the specialist in Birmingham on September 13, 2007. I called our friend, David, at Christ Church International. He told me to come right before they started service. One of the brothers spoke a prophetic word over me as we were praying. I'd heard similar words in my bedroom before I received the news about the lymphoma. How could the brother have known? God had spoken and was confirming what He told me. Oh, the comfort I felt. God loved me so much that He wanted to reassure me that He was with me. Call on your righteous elders.

Call on your prayer partners. Remember, we don't have to have a special title to pray for ourselves or others. I am blessed to be a part of a Small Group that understands the value of prayer. These ladies will stop what they are doing and immediately go into prayer. It's great to pray with a group.

WHAT HAPPENS WHEN WE PRAY

When we pray, we acknowledge that God is our Father and He is holy. We want His kingdom to come and we want His will to be done on earth as it is in heaven. His will is good and perfect. We're asking for daily bread – not for tomorrow or next week, but every day (Luke 11:3). We're keeping it fresh because we depend on Him day by day. We deal with tomorrow when it comes. We're asking Him to forgive us of our sins just as we forgive others who sinned against us. Remember if we don't forgive men, then God will not forgive our transgressions (Matthew 6:15).

It is important to note that any time prayer becomes a constant part of our lives, we will be tempted. We have an enemy that is prowling like a roaring lion[24]. He's hungry and looking for someone to devour. And that "someone" doesn't have to be us. But when he tries, we don't have to be afraid because greater is He who is in us than he who is in the world (1 John 4:4).

There will be times when you don't know what to do. I experienced this when my bones ached after the first chemo treatment. I had never experienced that kind of pain. This was a side effect of the drug, Neulasta®. I took some Tylenol® and Fred rubbed my legs. As I rested in bed, I pondered if I wanted to continue the treatments. I didn't share what I was thinking with anyone, but questions were certainly rolling through my mind. *Is it going to be like this all the time? What about Christmas for the children? Will I die of lymphoma if I stop the chemo*

---

[24] 1 Peter 5:8

treatments? What should I do?

I informed my doctor about the pain. He told me to continue with the Tylenol®. I went ahead and took the second treatment. The same thing happened again and more. That was it for me. No more pondering. I talked to the Lord through prayer, received peace, and made the decision ... no more chemo. I informed my family. My daughter, Shalunda, didn't agree with my decision and said, "You're going to die."

I told her, "And you're going to get some insurance money."

I prayed and left it up to the Lord. With or without chemo, I believed His will would be done. Refusing chemo was a sure death sentence based on what I was told. My doctor's clinical notes played through my mind:

...projected long-term survival of between 60 and 80% with systemic therapy. ... The patient understands explicitly that she needs therapy, and it will ultimately be fatal without treatment ...and most importantly there is no guarantee of success.

But I prayed, had peace, and made my choice.

When we speak and pray the Word, we are coming into agreement with God, and His power is released to answer our prayers. God's Word is alive and powerful, sharper than a double-edged sword.

For the word of God is alive and active. Sharper than any double-edged sword, it penetrates even to dividing soul and spirit, joints and marrow; it judges the thoughts and attitudes of the heart.
Hebrews 4:12

Imagine the type of weapon described here. Nothing can stand against it. It's sharp all the way around. Hebrews 4:12-13 (MSG) says:

God means what he says. What he says goes. His powerful Word is sharp as a surgeon's scalpel, cutting through everything, whether doubt or defense, laying us open to listen and obey. Nothing and no one is impervious to God's Word. We can't get away from it – no matter what.

I prayed the scriptures and reminded God of what He said. It's not that He is absent-minded, but repeating scriptures caused me to remember what He said and strengthened my faith. He is a covenant-keeping God and He keeps his promises. Psalm 105:8 (AMP) says, "He has remembered His covenant forever, the word which He commanded and established to a thousand generations." He doesn't forget. Nor does He have a problem with us reminding Him of what He said (Isaiah 43:26).

PRAYER WORKS

Prayer works. I've experienced it many times. God answered my prayer to not be in labor for over five hours and not have an episiotomy with our second child. Prayer worked when my nephew had a high fever: my aunt gave the prescribed medications and they didn't work, so we prayed and his fever broke. Prayer worked when my uncle had a bowel obstruction. We were told he could die. He took his prescribed medications and they didn't work. We prayed and the dam broke, literally.

Prayer worked when I was treated for a golf-ball sized cyst on my ovary. Surgery was scheduled. Brother Russ, a member of our extended family, anointed and prayed for me. I went back to the doctor the day before surgery. The doctor examined me and said, "I don't feel it. It's gone."

I asked, "What are you talking about?"

He said, "The cyst is gone." No surgery!

Prayer works for any situation from A to Z. God is not limited by our situation. Read Robert's story:

Imagine you and a friend are traveling. You are pulled over by the police and informed that there had been a shooting outside an establishment you passed. The officer is permitted to search you, your friend, and your automobile. He finds a .38 pistol in the trunk of your car which had not been fired. You are let go and days later questioned and then you and your friend are arrested for the crime of capital murder, a felony offense. This is what happened to me. I knew I was innocent, so I hired an attorney and entered a plea of not guilty.

A jury trial convened and lasted for two days. My attorney informed me that the District Attorney offered a plea. I was tired of the whole ordeal and gave thought to it, just to get it over. Then a team member asked, "Why would you plead guilty to something you didn't do?" and encouraged me to continue the fight. On the second day of trial, the jury returned with a verdict of Criminally Negligent Homicide, a misdemeanor. When asked why the verdict, they said, "We did not know who to believe."

I later found out that while the jury had been out deliberating, a relative of the victim approached my attorney and said, "He didn't kill him. Somebody else there shot him. He was already dead when his car passed." The attorney went to inform the clerk, and when he returned, he could not find her. He told my family about the lady but he did not know who she was. He said if she could be found that he would ask for a new trial.

My family prayed, "Lord, let the lady be found. Tell her she has to come and tell it." God answered (several months later). The lady was found, but not before the sentence was passed. I was sentenced and ordered to serve twelve months in the County Jail. I applied for probation and it was denied.

My attorney filed a motion for a new trial and a hearing was held. The lady testified she had seen my car. She followed the car and saw that no shots were fired out of the window. She stopped and learned that the victim had been killed. She testified it would have been impossible for me to have fired a shot that killed the victim because he was already dead when I passed the scene of the incident.

When asked by the District Attorney, "Why did you come forth now?" the lady responded three times, "The Lord told me I had to come!" The attorney felt that the testimony from a relative of the victim made it highly probable that a jury would reach a decision of "not guilty", and I was entitled to a new trial so that I would be acquitted of the charge. That did not happen.

The trial judge failed to rule in the time allowed by law, which caused the motion to be automatically denied. I was allowed to stay on bond during the appeals. The appeals courts affirmed the conviction, but a motion to reconsider probation was filed with the Trial Judge and a hearing held. Testimonies and witnesses were heard and I was placed on probation for two years.

God was at work in Robert's situation. Although he did not get a new trial to have an opportunity to be acquitted of the charge, he still did not admit to the charge nor was he charged with capital murder. Sometimes the answer may not turn out as you expect, but know that God has a bigger picture and your best interest at heart.

COMMUNICATE WITH GOD

Prayer is taking whatever you are carrying and giving it to God. Our shoulders weren't built to carry the weight of life alone. Paul wrote in Philippians 4:6-7, "Do not be anxious about anything, but in every situation, by prayer and petition, with thanksgiving, present your requests to God. And the peace of God, which transcends all understanding, will guard your hearts and your minds in Christ Jesus." It's right there in scripture. Pray in every situation and the peace of God will guard our hearts and mind. The Message version says:

Don't fret or worry. Instead of worrying, pray. Let petitions and praises shape your worries into prayers, letting God know your concerns. Before you know it, a sense of God's wholeness, everything coming together for good, will come and settle you down. It's wonderful what happens when Christ displaces worry at the center of your life.

I want to pray right now (remember, you can pray anywhere, anytime): *Lord, thank You for the times You gave me peace during my storms. Thank You for providing me with a solid team who walked this journey with me. Thank You for using every healthcare provider, as well, allowing me to walk and get to this place.*

And Lord, I ask that everyone who reads this book will trust You and receive what You have purposed in their life as they travel their journey. Lord, we look to You. You are our hope and strength. You, alone, receive all the Glory. Amen!

THE SCRIPTURAL GUARANTEE

God *wants* us to remember what He promised and stand on it:

My covenant will I not break, nor alter the thing that is gone out of my lips.
Psalms 89:34 KJV

Everything we need is in the covenant (Hebrews 8:6). Healing is under the covenant and I needed it. One thing always caught my attention as I searched the scriptures: there were many instances where Jesus healed people. They brought anybody with an ailment, whether mental, emotional, or physical, to Jesus. He healed them, one and all.

Jesus went through Galilee, teaching in their synagogues, proclaiming the good news of the kingdom, and healing every disease and sickness among the people. News about him spread all over Syria, and people brought to him all who were ill with various diseases, those suffering severe pain, the demon-possessed, those having seizures, and the paralyzed; and he healed them. Large crowds from Galilee, the Decapolis, Jerusalem, Judea and the region across the Jordan followed him.
Matthew 4:23-25

Jesus was always willing to heal people. He was just waiting for them to come to Him. Have you heard of the two blind men who sat beside the road as Jesus walked by? They heard that Jesus was coming and cried out, "Have mercy on us, Son of David!" The crowd told them to be silent, but they got louder. They didn't stop. Jesus asked the men, "Do you believe that I am able to do this?"

"Yes, Lord," they replied. Jesus touched their eyes and said, "According to your faith let it be done to you," and they were healed (Matthew 9:27-30).

There are other instances of Jesus' willingness to deliver, set free, and heal. He hasn't changed. He's still waiting for us to come to Him. We no longer have to sit around and die. I am reminded of the four lepers in 2 Kings 7 as they sat outside the city gate having a conversation.

...What are we doing sitting here at death's door? If we enter the famine-struck city we'll die; if we stay here we'll die. So let's take our chances in the camp of Aram and throw ourselves on their mercy. If they receive us we'll live, if they kill us we'll die. We've got nothing to lose.
2 Kings 7:3-4 MSG

Pause Break – Pause Break!

So, what are you waiting for? You don't have to stay where you are. Go and search the scriptures and pray. If you've been given man's report on anything, choose to believe the report of the Lord. You have nothing to lose.

Don't be like the attendant who said to Elisha, "You expect us to believe that? Trap doors opening in the sky and food tumbling out?" Elisha told the attendant that because of his unbelief, he'd watch it with his own eyes but would not eat so much as a mouthful. The crowd trampled over him while coming through the city gate to get some food. He got exactly what he believed and you will, too[25]. That is why you should search and believe the promises.

You have the choice to sit and die or go in and find what you need. Here are a few promises that encouraged me:

---

[25] 2 Kings 7:2, 18-20 MSG

...I am watching to see that my word is fulfilled.
Jeremiah 1:12

...Ask and you will receive, and your joy will be complete.
John 16:24

If you believe, you will receive whatever you ask for in prayer.
Matthew 21:22

You may ask me for anything in my name, and I will do it.
John 14:14

...The prayer of a righteous person is powerful and effective.
James 5:16

The righteous cry out, and the LORD hears them; he delivers them from all their troubles.
Psalm 34:17

You will pray to him, and he will hear you. ...
Job 22:27

This is the confidence we have in approaching God: that if we ask anything according to his will, he hears us.
1 John 5:14

And I will do whatever you ask in my name, so that the Father may be glorified in the Son.
John 14:13

He will call on me, and I will answer him; I will be with him in trouble. I will deliver him and honor him.
Psalms 91:15

Take these promises and say them out loud. Keep saying them until they become life for you. That's prayer! Write them down and strategically place copies (even sticky notes) all around so they are constantly before your eyes. I posted them in every room in my house, including the bathroom. No room was off-limits.

Psalm 145:18-19 (AMP) says, "The Lord is near to all who call on Him, To all who call on Him in truth (without guile). He will fulfill the desire of those who fear and worship Him [with awe-inspired reverence and obedience]; He also will hear their cry and will save them." This should encourage us to pray.

Prayer is vital. It's our secret weapon that's not a secret. We can use it anytime and anywhere. No situation is off-limits. That's the kind of God we serve: a God who tells us we don't have to be anxious about anything. A God who beckons us to call on Him and He will answer.

Call Him. There is no call waiting, call forwarding, being placed on hold, or talking to an automated voice. He will answer. He said, "Call to me, and I will answer you" (Jeremiah 33:3).

If you want your circumstances to change, then do what you must do, search the scriptures, and commit to pray. No more excuses or feeling sorry for yourself. Get up! God has already done His part. He is willing and waiting for us to do ours.

May we be intentional, persistent, and pray.

---------------**6**----------------

WILLING TO WALK BY FAITH
"For we live by faith, not by sight." 2 Corinthians 5:7

Most of us have heard of faith and have some idea what it is. Faith is a firm persuasion and expectation that God will perform all He promised to us in Jesus Christ. It is not based on what we see or human reasoning (what we think). Faith comes when we focus our attention on God and His Word. It does not look at the calendar but to the Lord. It does not look at the diagnosis but to the Lord. Faith will endure until it is replaced by the thing that we believe for comes into existence. We set ourselves up for failure, pain, and eventual defeat when we stop having faith in God and His promises.

I have seen people go through difficulties. They, and others around them, discuss their situation more than believing in God. You ask how they're doing and they say:

"Well, the doctor said..."

"It hasn't gotten any better..."

"They're trying something new..."

"I'm just holding on..."

Then, after magnifying the situation, God may get one measly mention: "I keep praying to God though." You *know* I am telling the truth. We have probably been guilty of the same thing. Shame on us.

God gave each of us a measure of faith (Romans 12:3). He does not show favoritism. [29] The measure we were given when we received Jesus as Savior and Lord was enough to cause us to be born again. And it is enough to bring victory over

---

[29] Acts 10:34

anything that comes our way.

This is the confidence we have in approaching God: that if we ask anything according to his will, he hears us. And if we know that he hears us – whatever we ask – we know that we have what we asked of him.
1 John 5:14-15

FAITH AND HOPE

We often use the words "faith" and "hope" interchangeably. Hope believes that our future is good, even if our present is bad.

Against all hope, Abraham in hope believed and so became the father of many nations, just as it had been said to him, "So shall your offspring be." Without weakening in his faith, he faced the fact that his body was as good as dead – since he was about a hundred years old – and that Sarah's womb was also dead. Yet he did not waver through unbelief regarding the promise of God, but was strengthened in his faith and gave glory to God, being fully persuaded that God had power to do what he had promised. This is why it was credited to him as righteousness.
Romans 4:18-22

Our souls must have hope, just as our bodies must have the energy to keep going. Psalm 33:18 says, "But the eyes of the Lord are on those who fear him, on those whose hope is in his unfailing love." Psalm 31:24 reminds us that as we hope in the Lord, we can be of good courage because He strengthens our hearts. He is our hiding place and shield (Psalm 119:114).

Hebrews 11:1 (KJV) says, "Now faith is the substance of things hoped for, the evidence of things not seen." In other words, faith is both the substance of things hoped for and the evidence that things exist that are not yet perceived with the senses. My faith could have been shaken after hearing the words, "... I feel she really must receive systemic chemotherapy followed by involved field radiotherapy and possibly consolidation with a high-dose therapy and autologous stem cell transplantation."

Pause Break – Pause Break!

Faith calls those things that be not as though they were. In other words, it acts like you have it before you actually get it. We act in faith when we expect a paycheck from our employer. Why is it that we have a problem believing our all-powerful God can handle our issues? We have to be willing to walk by faith and not by sight.

I didn't have my healing in the natural yet, but I kept remembering what the Lord said: "Don't be moved by what you hear." He already knew there would be many voices speaking into my ears that would question my faith, so He gave me a blessed assurance to stand firm on what I believed. This calls for another prayer moment (remember, anywhere, anytime!): *Thank you, Lord, for protecting my mind and allowing me to stand as these words were spoken. You loved me so much and gave me assurance and peace. I love You!*

USING FAITH

The Lord honors those who have faith in Him. I've seen it. I witnessed a friend named Dot as she battled throat cancer. At that time, I had only been a Christian for less than six months. The Lord told me to go and tell her that He could heal her of cancer. So, I went. "Dot, the Lord told me to come and tell you that he could heal you of your cancer," I said.

She didn't respond.

"Do you believe him?" I asked.

She began to cry. I thought I had done something wrong.

"I am going to go now," I said. As I prepared to leave, I heard the Lord say, "Pray for her." I was stunned for a second, and then I said, "Dot, the Lord told me to pray for you. I don't know what to pray but I guess He'll have to tell me what to say." I don't know what I prayed but I remember feeling different when I left. Oh, the innocence and simplicity of those days – just doing what He said without reservations. I later called and asked Dot to go to a revival with me. She said yes and off we went. Those in need of prayer were asked to come to the altar. To my surprise, Dot got in the line. At the completion of the altar call, Evangelist Williams said, "God has done something mighty for someone tonight."

Dot had returned from the altar showing no emotions at all but she jumped up when the evangelist spoke. "It was me. It was me. I had cancer and God healed me of cancer!" Dot shouted.

I lost it and had a hallelujah-good shouting time! You have to understand that Dot is shy, like shy-shy. It was the power of God operating in her because she would have never stood up in a public forum. That's just not Dot.

Dot and I talked later. She told me she wasn't going to her doctor's appointment. I told her I thought she should so that they would know. She agreed and went to her appointment.

"Are you ready for treatment?" the technician asked.

"I don't have cancer anymore," she said.

"Who told you that?" he asked.

"God healed me," she said.

Scans were taken and guess what? No cancer was found. She didn't even flinch when told, "We've seen this kind go away but it can come back."

Dot took the Lord at His word. She believed Him when He told her, "I can heal you of your cancer." Dot operated in faith and – 35 years later – is still cancer-free.

We must have faith. It is impossible to please Him without it. We have to have it.

CHARACTERISTICS OF FAITH

Believing God requires that we walk by faith and not by sight. Truly understanding what faith is and how powerful it can be will help you know for sure if you're walking by faith and not sight. Here are three important characteristics of faith:

Faith is progressive. Just like breathing, belief is not designed to be a one-time event or confession of faith, but rather a continual state of trusting in the Lord. We demonstrate it through our actions and words.

Faith is not stagnant. We can't sit around. We have to move – do something. Act on what we hear. We can't walk around in unbelief or focus our attention on anything contrary to what the Lord has said. This would be like the person described in James 1:8: double-minded, unstable, and restless in everything he thinks, feels, or decides. There is no peace in this state. Faith without action is dead (James 2:17). Our actions speak volumes.

Don't fool yourself into thinking that you are a listener when you are anything but, letting the Word go in one ear and out the other. Act on what you hear! Those who hear and don't act are like those who glance in the mirror, walk away, and two minutes later have no idea who they are, what they look like. But whoever catches a glimpse of the revealed counsel of God – the free life! – even out of the corner of his eye, and sticks with it, is no distracted scatterbrain but a man or woman of action. That person will find delight and affirmation in the action.
James 1:22-25 MSG

Faith is settled. If the prophet, Elijah, was here, he would ask the same question he asked in 1 King 18:21 (AMP), "…How long will you hesitate between two opinions? If the Lord is God, follow Him; but if Baal, follow him." Take a stand. God is God or He's not. We can't continue to falter between two opinions and expect to receive anything from Him.

ALL IS WELL

What do we really want? Whatever we magnify becomes

bigger. So, if we want our situation to change, we need to magnify God. He has no limits and has the power to turn it around. Jesus said, "...The work of God is this: to believe in the one he has sent" (John 6:29). No wonder the enemy tries to divert us from believing. He knows he loses his hold on us when we start acting on our beliefs. This is why it is so important to stay before the Lord and get a proper diet of the Word.

My doctor would always ask, "Ms. Wimes, how are you doing?"

I would always say, "All is well." It didn't matter if I didn't look well. I was walking by faith and not being moved by how I felt or what I heard. You'll notice – as I said in the introduction – that "All is well" and the explanation behind it was a repetitive state for me. It was intentional.

I heard what was said: *no more than 45-50% and you may end up needing a bone marrow transplant or more aggressive measures; development of other types of cancers appears to be in a complete remission radiographically, although the PET scan is a little less certain approximately;* 30% *of long-term disease-free survival.*

The constant changes appeared to be circumstantial, like evidence in a court of law. Circumstantial evidence against someone may not be enough but it can contribute to other decisions made concerning the case. Despite the evidence, I was sticking to God's (which became my) verdict and wasn't being moved by what I heard.

"All Is Well" became my theme song. These three words allowed me the opportunity to encourage and share about the Shunammite woman in 2 Kings 4:8-37. Her son was out in the field with his daddy until he complained that his head was hurting. His daddy sent him to his mother. He laid on her lap and died. He was her only child. But it didn't end there.

She went up and laid him on the bed of the man of God, and shut the door [of the small upper room] behind him and left. Then she called to her husband and said, "Please send me one of the servants and one of the donkeys, so that I may run to the man of God and return." He

said, "Why are you going to him today? It is neither the New Moon nor the Sabbath." And she said, "It will be all right." Then she saddled the donkey and said to her servant, "Drive [the animal] fast; do not slow down the pace for me unless I tell you." So she set out and came to the man of God at Mount Carmel. ...
2 Kings 4:21-25 AMP

Did you notice the woman didn't even tell her husband their son was dead? I wondered why. What if he knew? How do you think he would have responded? Would he have allowed her to go to the man of God? Would he think she was crazy thinking the man of God could bring their son back to life? Maybe she knew her husband and felt it was better not to tell him. How would you have handled this situation? Have you had times when you've kept things to yourself? I have. I didn't want to share about the cancer with anyone that I didn't feel should know. I especially didn't want to tell my mother because she worries "Worry" to no end. But I knew they would somehow hear about it. So, I figured they might as well hear it from me.

The Shunammite woman was unique. It doesn't appear that she went into a panic mode, crying and screaming, "My son is dead. My son is dead!" She had a plan. I'm not sure what she looked like when she approached the man of God but it drew his attention.

...When the man of God saw her at a distance, he said to Gehazi his servant, "Look, there is the Shunammite woman. Please run now to meet her and ask her, 'Is it well with you? Is it well with your husband? Is it well with the child?'" And she answered, "It is well."
2 Kings 4:25-26 AMP

Remember, this woman's son was dead. Yet she responds, "It is well," everything is all right, and all is well. If she could say that, *knowing* her son was dead, then surely, I could say it, too. After all, I was still alive (even if some thought I was dead).

Jairus, a synagogue official in the Bible, came and fell at Jesus' feet begging Him to come to his house because his only daughter was dying. While he was still speaking, someone from his house came and said, "Your daughter is dead; do not inconvenience the Teacher any further." Jesus heard them and said, "Do not be afraid any longer; only believe and trust [in Me and have faith in My ability to do this], and she will be made well" (Luke 8:49-50 AMP). Jairus kept believing. Jesus went to his house, took his daughter by the hand, told her to get up, and she stood up.

Jesus saw the widow of Nain in a funeral procession for her only son (Luke 7:11-15). He felt compassion and told her not to weep. He went to the casket and told her son to arise from the dead. He sat up and began to speak. The widow got her son back.

Your faith will be tested just as Jairus and the widow. If you're hoping for something and then you receive a negative report, keep on believing. Keep walking and hang in there no matter what it looks like. It's only a test.

GUARANTEED TESTING

Our whole life is one big test. We test to obtain a permit. We test to become a legal driver. We test to graduate from school. We test to practice medicine or law. Test, test, and more tests on top of the tests! James says:

Consider it nothing but joy, my brothers and sisters, whenever you fall into various trials. Be assured that the testing of your faith [through experience] produces endurance [leading to spiritual maturity, and inner peace].
James 1:2-3 AMP

Blessed [happy, spiritually prosperous, favored by God] is the man who is steadfast under trial and perseveres when tempted; for when he has passed the test and been approved, he will receive the [victor's]

crown of life which the Lord has promised to those who love Him.
James 1:12 AMP

Here is what I've learned: Expect the tests, tribulation, and persecution. It's part of life and they're coming.

I have told you these things, so that in me you may have peace. In this world you will have trouble. But take heart! I have overcome the world.
John 16:33

In fact, everyone who wants to live a godly life in Christ Jesus will be persecuted.
2 Timothy 3:12

Remember what I told you: 'A servant is not greater than his master.' If they persecuted me, they will persecute you also. If they obeyed my teaching, they will obey yours also.
John 15:20

The righteous person may have many troubles, but the Lord delivers him from them all.
Psalm 34:19

I felt like I was on trial in a court of law when my testing started with cancer. The "prosecutor" (the doctor in my case) presented his case. The "jury" (the medical team) went into deliberation and came back with a verdict (diagnosis). And boy did they come back with one: "It's Cancer ... non-Hodgkin's Lymphoma."

I didn't have to appeal the verdict. The Supreme Judge (God) had already said, "Don't be moved by what you hear." He has the final ruling in my life.

We have an enemy competing for our faith. He's a bully. What do we do when we're being bullied? I don't know about you, but I fight back using the Word and my faith. Why would we allow that bully to take what is rightfully ours? Go down fighting. Don't give in or up! The fight is on and we win as long as we don't give in. We've got to stop allowing him to run roughshod over us.

Even a baby takes ownership of his or her bottle. Just try taking it away. We should be the same way. Find what is yours. Search the scriptures.

We have to study to prepare for the test. Hosea 4:6 speaks of God's people being destroyed for the lack of knowledge. We have sat on our blessed assurance long enough. It's time to dive into the Word. Jesus said to those who believed on him that if they continue in his word, then they are his disciples indeed, and they will know the truth and the truth shall make them free (John 8:31-32). *They will know the truth*. What is the truth? Whatever God says. That's why we study. Everything in Christ Jesus is ours. It's our inheritance.

Did we not study for tests in school? If we did, then why would we think we don't have to study the Word to be equipped for the tests we will encounter? The beauty of our test is that we don't have to face it alone. Psalm 23:4 reminds us, "Even though I walk through the darkest valley, I will fear no evil, for you are with me; your rod and your staff, they comfort me." God is with and for us.

EXAMINATION TIME

Some have said I had great faith. I don't know about that. I was simply walking and believing what I heard the Lord say: "Don't be moved by what you hear." And then I studied for my test. I looked up every scripture I could find concerning healing and reminded myself of who I was and to whom I belonged. I learned to take every thought captive, to make sure the enemy had no advantage over me in the battle for control of my mind. There are many times – even now – when the thought of the cancer coming back crosses my mind. I just continue to remind myself of the scriptures. If it's not a thought that aligns itself with the Word, I immediately put it under arrest and send it to prison for life. I don't even give it a pardon. I do this as many times as it tries to get an appeal.

Your faith grows when you are confident in the outcome of the things for which you believe. Second Corinthians 10:5 says, "We demolish arguments and every pretension that sets itself up against the knowledge of God, and we take captive every thought to make it obedient to Christ." Just follow His instructions and leave the results up to Him.

Shadrach, Meshach, and Abednego were in a situation involving God and their faith. They were willing to die for their belief. Their partner, Daniel, was thrown in the lions' den. These young men could have taken the easy way out and given in, but they were committed to God to the point of death. The King recognized that Daniel was a servant of the living God. When Daniel survived the lion's den, the king asked, "Daniel, servant of the living God, has your God, whom you serve continually, been able to rescue you from the lions?" (Daniel 6:20). What a testimony. Would the world recognize that *we* serve God?

Here's another powerful piece of scripture. James 1:2-4 reminds us that tests are going to happen, but that we should actually be happy about it. Here's why: "testing of your faith produces patience," and as a perfect work, patience allows us to be perfect and complete and without lack. Do you believe this?

Let's take a look at Job. God bragged about how Job was the finest man in all the earth, a complete man of integrity. God said Job feared Him and stayed away from evil. God allowed Satan to put Job to the test. The first test was Satan's attempt to take away all of Job's animals, killing the servants that were with the animals, and killing all of Job's sons and daughters while they were eating together[31]. Even though Satan did these things to Job's belongings, Job did not curse God like Satan wanted him to do. What Satan meant for evil turned out for Job's good:

---

[31] Job 1

After Job prayed for his friends, the Lord restored his fortunes and gave him twice as much as he had before. All his brothers and sisters and everyone who knew him before came and ate with him in his house. They comforted and consoled him over all the trouble the Lord brought upon him, and each one gave him a piece of silver and a gold ring. The Lord blessed the latter part of Job's life more than the former part: he was given 14,000 sheep, 6,000 camels, 1,000 yoke of oxen and 1,000 donkeys. He also had seven sons and three daughters. After this, Job lived a hundred and forty years; he saw his children and their children to the fourth generation.
Job 42:10-16

Will the Lord be able to say, "Have you considered my servant *(place your name here)*?" That's a hard question, isn't it? It should make us ponder and hopefully examine our walk with the Lord. There is no test or trial that we won't get through or pass as long as we keep our faith in the Lord.

A STUDY GUIDE FOR GREAT FAITH

I learned that with a few matter-of-fact strategies in all circumstances, our faith builds to a point where peace rises to the top and God's power always prevails. Here are some notes on each:

You have to start in order to finish. Peter did not begin to sink until he took his eyes off Jesus (Matthew 14:28-33). He looked at the circumstances around him – the strong wind and waves. When he realized he was sinking, he called out to the Lord for help. Now, let's not be too hard on Peter because he at least got out of the boat and walked on the water. Some of us are hesitant to get in or out of the boat, much less walk on the water. You have to start somewhere. Get up. Start walking. Then, if you feel like you're starting to sink, call on Jesus.

My family and I had the opportunity to "get out of the boat" many times and experience the strong winds and waves. It came time to walk on the water and have CT scans performed on December 28, 2007. The results were:

(1) No CT evidence of intrathoracic lymphoma of the Chest,

(2) Marked interval improvement. No lymphadenopathy by CT size criteria of the Neck,

(3) No evidence of lymphoma in the abdomen or pelvis. Accessory splenic tissue is stable.

I went back to my appointment on January 16, 2008. My doctor wrote:

On examination, she was well. Ms. Wimes is clinically well and has recovered from her chemotherapy (with the exception of her hair growth). She appears to be in a complete remission radiographically, although the PET scan is a little less certain. It is not definitive for residual disease, but I am anxious about this. I discussed with Ms. Wimes and her husband at length. She has not had adequate therapy, so she has not completed adequate therapy to give her a high enough chance of cure, and I was quite straight with her about this. I was worried that with the residual abnormalities on the CT and PET scan, while there has clearly been an excellent response, I feel she should be consolidated with two further cycles of CHOP, and preferably four further cycles of CHOP. She and her husband voiced clear understanding. She understands the implications of refusing more therapy, but does not want any more treatment at this time and wants to get on with her work. I told her that I did not think that she would be good to her ministry if we are not able to cure her of her lymphoma. She did understand this, but is not willing to take anymore therapy. She voiced understanding as to this, and made clear that this was her decision, she did not want to go on.

I couldn't believe the doctor's report if I wanted to because nothing seemed to be concrete. I appeared to be in a complete remission radiographically, although the PET scan in 2007 was a little less certain. It was not definite for residual disease. Residual disease is cancer cells that remain after attempts to remove the cancer have been made. Did the PET scan see something or didn't it? This was still too confusing.

We kept walking by faith. I was at peace and determined not to be moved. I kept my routine and kept on walking. I was in a good place, constantly remembering what the Lord said, and I was leaving the results up to Him. I felt like Esther: if I perished, I perished (Esther 4:16). I was trusting the Lord even if it meant death. After all, what did I have to lose?

Don't be moved. Recognize it for what it is. It's just a test: a test of your faith. It's like the interruption on our TV screen when it displays "THIS IS ONLY A TEST." We don't try to figure it out. We let it run its course and the program returns. It was only a test.

Don't get lost in the format of life's exams. Testing interrupts our lives. Don't try to figure them out. Continue to walk by faith and trust God. Don't be moved by the hard questions. There are examples of people whose faith was tested in Hebrews 11. We call them the heroes of faith. These people sacrificed and some of them died for their faith.

All these people were still living by faith when they died. They did not receive the things promised; they only saw them and welcomed them from a distance, admitting that they were foreigners and strangers on earth. People who say such things show that they are looking for a country of their own. If they had been thinking of the country they had left, they would have had opportunity to return. Instead, they were longing for a better country – a heavenly one. Therefore God is not ashamed to be called their God, for he has prepared a city for them. Hebrews 11:13-16

These heroes were still living by faith at the time they died. And God was not ashamed to be called their God. Some were put in prison, put to death by stoning, sawed in two and killed by the sword. They were persecuted and mistreated.

These were all commended for their faith, yet none of them received what had been promised, since God had planned something better for us so that only together with us would they be made perfect. Hebrews 11:39-40

You may say, "Yeah, but they're all dead. What can they tell me?" I get it. Let me tell you about some who are still living. By faith:

A young man diagnosed with brain cancer was given three to four months to live and now is alive and well.

A lady, who walked through cancer alone and received a word from the Lord to live is still alive, too.

A young lady who chose to believe a word from God stopped treatment and was healed of throat cancer, and remains cancer-free.

A young lady, healed of colon cancer, remains healed.

And then there's me. I was given about a 30% survival rate but was healed of non-Hodgkin's Lymphoma (and I'm still kicking).

These aren't testimonies that I heard or read about. I have personally been involved with and witnessed every one of them. God shows up on behalf of those who take Him at His Word. He is real, He is a healer, He is a deliverer, and He honors those who walk by faith.

Our faith has to be settled. Do we believe God even when we're in pain and suffering? Do we believe the promises of God even when everything looks impossible? Now for the big question: are you willing to *die* for what you believe? It could very well come to that. And if it does, are you ready to meet Him? If not, take a look back at Chapter One's first Pause Break – Pause Break for a quick prayer on salvation.

Take God at His Word, operate in faith, believe that He is and that He rewards those who diligently seek Him[32]. Search and see what the Word has to say. Feed on the Word and grow, and leave the results up to Him. Remember: we walk by faith and not by sight!

---

[32] Hebrews 11:6

--------------------7--------------------

WILLING TO NOT LIMIT GOD

*Yea, they turned back and tempted God, and limited the Holy
One of Israel.* Psalm 78:41 KJV

Can man limit God? You're probably thinking there is no way.
He's God! He has all power. And that is true. God's power is
not limited. He is supreme and can do anything, and He wants
to do anything for you that you ask. But it is also true that *we*
can place limits on the blessings He brings into *our* lives. We do
it and sometimes without even knowing it. We restrict or
confine Him within our self-imposed boundaries. We have to
take the limits off in order to witness the flow of God in our
lives.

There are times we're like a jar with a lid on it. It's confined
in the sense that nothing can get in or come out because the
limit (or tightened lid) is placed. We oftentimes treat God the
same: nothing in, nothing out. It's time to take a self-
examination and look at our behavior. Let's also observe others
and learn from them.

In the book of Mark, Jesus was in His own country on the
Sabbath teaching in the synagogue. Many heard Him and
were astonished. They asked, "Where did this man get these
things?" "What's this wisdom that has been given him?" "Is
this not the carpenter, the Son of Mary, and brother of James,
Joseph, Judas, and Simon? And are not His sisters here with
us?" (Mark 6:2-6). The crowd saw a carpenter – Mary's boy.
Their minds tripped over what little they knew about Him and
never got any further. Without even realizing it, they limited
God. Instead of seeing the big picture, they got caught up in the
details. They were offended. As a result, Mark 6:5 says Jesus

could do no mighty work there. All He did was lay His hands on a few sick people and heal them. I wonder the number of people who could have received their miracle if only they had believed and not limited Him. Or better yet, imagine if you were among those few who could not get healed because of the lack of belief? Jesus marveled because of their unbelief.

Have you ever tried to get through to a person who was offended? It's not an easy task because they are confined within themselves about their belief on what or who caused the offense. Proverbs 18:19 (AMP) says, "A brother offended is harder to win over than a fortified city..."

In Numbers, God told Moses to send men to scout out the land of Canaan that He was giving to the Israelites. Moses sent out 12 spies with specific instructions:

... "Go up through the Negev and on into the hill country. See what the land is like and whether the people who live there are strong or weak, few or many. What kind of land do they live in? Is it good or bad? What kind of towns do they live in? Are they unwalled or fortified? How is the soil? Is it fertile or poor? Are there trees in it or not? Do your best to bring back some of the fruit of the land. ...
Numbers 13:17-20

The spies went and returned with their report. Ten of the men came back with more information than requested. They said,

"We can't attack those people; they are stronger than we are." And they spread among the Israelites a bad report about the land they had explored. They said, "The land we explored devours those living in it. All the people we saw there are of great size. We saw the Nephilim there (the descendants of Anak come from the Nephilim). We seemed like grasshoppers in our own eyes, and we looked the same to them."
Numbers 13:31-33

Who told the spies they looked like grasshoppers? Was it the Nephilim? No. It was their self-imposed limitations.

The other two spies, Caleb and Joshua, didn't impose any limitations. They believed they could go up and take possession of the land. They saw the same giants and weren't moved by the sight of them. They believed in God.

...The land we passed through and explored is exceedingly good. If the Lord is pleased with us, he will lead us into that land, a land flowing with milk and honey, and will give it to us. Only do not rebel against the Lord. And do not be afraid of the people of the land, because we will devour them. Their protection is gone, but the Lord is with us. Do not be afraid of them.
Numbers 14:7-9

However, the ten spies' bad report caused the others to raise their voices and weep aloud. They grumbled against Moses and Aaron. And imagine this: they wanted another leader and to go back to Egypt (Numbers 14:1-4)! Remember, God already promised the land to them[37], but their minds – with the help of Ruthlessness, Bitterness, Misery, Suffering and Broken Spirit – introduced them to an alternative. Had they lost their minds and forgotten what it was like being in slavery? They limited God because they forgot His identity as their miracle-working God: the same God who delivered them out of Egypt. The same God who drowned Pharaoh's whole army in the sea.

Now, the others had an opportunity to change their minds. They were told not to rebel against the Lord or fear the people of the land because the Lord was with them. But yet, they turned a deaf ear, opposed, and disobeyed God. They didn't listen. The Lord considered what they did as contempt. He said, "... as surely as I live and as surely as the glory of the Lord fills the whole earth, not one of those who saw my glory and the

---

[37] Exodus 3:17

signs I performed in Egypt and in the wilderness but who disobeyed me and tested me ten times—not one of them will ever see the land I promised on oath to their ancestors. No one who has treated me with contempt will ever see it" (Numbers 14:21-23).

The word "contempt" is a strong word. We often hear it used in a courtroom. People who are held in contempt are usually fined or incarcerated. How could the Israelites have no respect for God after all He had done for them?

Psalm 78:10 says the Israelites did not keep the covenant of God and refused to walk in His law. As a result, all the children of Israel – except Caleb and Joshua – who were 20 years old and older died in the wilderness and did not enter the promised land: "Yea, they turned back and tempted God, and limited the Holy One of Israel" (Psalm 78:41 KJV).

TRUSTING GOD TO KEEP HIS WORD

God can't break His Word, and because His word cannot change, His promises are likewise unchangeable. He says it and He does it every time. The Word of God stands forever (Isaiah 40:8). God said, "So will My word be which goes out of My mouth; It will not return to Me void (useless, without result), Without accomplishing what I desire, And without succeeding in the matter for which I sent it" (Isaiah 55:11 AMP). I don't know about you, but I am so grateful that God is nothing like us.

Pause Break – Pause Break!

Don't rush. Just mark your page and come back to it. I am still in awe when I think that all God is asking is that we believe: to take Him at His Word and allow His power to be manifested. Why would we place Him in a jar with a lid on it or in a box?

We must stop judging Him based on our circumstances or experiences. He has always done just what He said He would do. Numbers 23:19 (AMP) says, "God is not a man, that He should lie, Nor a son of man, that He should repent. Has He said, and will He not do it? Or has He spoken and will He not make it good and fulfill it?" Second Timothy 2:13 reminds us that even when we are faithless, He remains faithful because He cannot deny Himself. When you look at the Israelites, are we any different? Are we divided in our opinions? How often have we been in contempt?

Say this prayer: *Lord, help us trust You and take You at Your Word. Help us not to rebel and limit You. Okay, we can move on now.*

Notice children after being promised a new toy. They tell others, "My daddy (or mommy, friend, or grandparent) is going to buy me a toy." They don't question or even think whether the person has the means to make it happen. They take them at their word. Why? Because they believe in and trust the one who promised.

We witnessed this at one of our Christmas parties for our prison ministry. Several children looked forward to our giveaway of a guitar for a Nintendo Wii Rock Band system. We overheard one boy say to another child waiting for the announcement, "You don't even have a Wii."

When I heard it, I asked the child if he had the system. He said, "I don't have one, but my daddy said he was going to buy it for me."

Now get this: his daddy wasn't gainfully employed. He was incarcerated. How *could* he buy it? To the child, it didn't matter. This child did not place a limit on his daddy or his confinement. It made no difference. Daddy said he would get it and that was enough for the child. (And by the way, the little boy got the guitar *and* a Wii system that Christmas.)

How do we respond when our circumstances don't look favorable? Do we still believe in God? Can you imagine how God would feel if we believed and took Him at His Word like the child did his parent?

USING OUR WORDS (AND ACTIONS) WISELY

Our words will work for or against us. Proverbs 18:21 says, "The tongue has the power of life and death, and those who love it will eat its fruit." What we say can preserve or destroy our life. Our words are like the steering wheel of a car. The car goes whichever way we turn the steering wheel. James 3:3-5 says, "When we put bits into the mouths of horses to make them obey us, we can turn the whole animal. Or, take ships as an example. Although they are so large and are driven by strong winds, they are steered by a very small rudder wherever the pilot wants to go. Likewise, the tongue is a small part of the body, but it makes great boasts. Consider what a great forest is set on fire by a small spark."

We will be acquitted or condemned by our words (Matthew 12:37), so it's important to know why we say what we say when we want what we want. Jesus told us, "... for out of the abundance of the heart the mouth speaketh" (Matthew 12:34 KJV).

Our word, not someone else's, will free us from a criminal charge by a verdict of "not guilty," so we need to look deeper into our hearts and change its condition. Don't forget the Israelites. They said, "...If only we had died in Egypt! Or in this wilderness!" Guess what? No, don't guess. Just go read Numbers 14.

Another example can be found with King Saul. God told him to go, attack the Amalekites and totally destroy all that belonged to them. Saul was not to spare them and instead was to put to death men and women, children and infants, cattle and sheep, camels and donkeys" (1 Samuel 15:3). Well, Saul did not follow all of God's instructions and instead ordered his own action plan. He took Agag, king of the Amalekites, alive and the best of the sheep, the oxen, the fatlings, the lambs, and all that was good and did not destroy them. God saw it and sent Samuel with a word for Saul.

When Samuel reached him, Saul said, "The Lord bless you! I have carried out the Lord's instructions." But Samuel said, "What then is this bleating of sheep in my ears? What is this lowing of cattle that I hear?"
1 Samuel 15:13-14

Saul actually thought he had an excuse to disobey. He blamed the soldiers, but aimed to confirm they meant well in their actions: "The soldiers brought them from the Amalekites; they spared the best of the sheep and cattle to sacrifice to the Lord your God, but we totally destroyed the rest" (1 Samuel 15:15).

Saul was the King and in charge, not the soldiers. He had an option to order what God said. Neither Saul's excuse – nor his intent – held up. He was disobedient by failing to totally obey God. God regretted He set him as king. Saul limited God by his disobedience and lost his kingship.

What's our excuse? Are we limiting God because of our unbelief, fear, what we are saying, forgetting, expectations, or just plain disobedience?

TAKE THE LIMITS OFF

Jesus said, "…Verily I say unto you, If ye have faith, and doubt not, ye shall not only do this which is done to the fig tree, but also if ye shall say unto this mountain, Be thou removed, and be thou cast into the sea; it shall be done" (Matthew 21:21 KJV). If you believe this in your heart, your words will line up with God's word. That's exactly what I did when I was told the cancer had come back. I spoke to that mountain and said, "Ain't no cancer come back." How could I say that when a doctor said the cancer had indeed come back? I had to believe in my heart what God said. There was never any indication of cancer on my right side. I was not changing what I knew, nor was I willing to alter what I knew God said.

The more we say something, the more we will believe it. And the more we believe it, the more we will say it. We have to agree with the Word and speak only words we want to come to pass.

Let's use our mouth as a thermostat and not a thermometer. The thermometer *measures* the situation, but the thermostat *changes* the situation. A thermometer reflects the temperature of the environment. It reacts to what's happening around it. If the temperature is hot, it tells you so. If it's cold, the thermometer reflects that reality, as well. In contrast, a thermostat regulates the environment. It sets the desired temperature of the room and actively works to maintain it within a given range. It makes the decision to correct situations. If the temperature rises above the goal, the thermostat signals the air conditioner to crank up and cool the room down. If the temperature falls below the goal, the thermostat causes the heater to turn on to warm the room. Jesus used his words as a thermostat. No limitations. He wasn't moved by the environment. He was obedient and said only what He heard God say. Let's imitate Him and do the same.

Listening and obeying God over everything else keeps God's flow in our lives. Disobedience, failure, or refusal to obey limits God. I would have limited God had I not listened to what He said and been moved by what I was hearing. I am not convinced that I would still be alive if I didn't choose this course of action. The constant changes were enough to cause me to worry myself to death.

Again, what we say has a lot to do with our heart condition. Even in our well-meaning of facing what we experience ("if the doctor said it, I need to honor his or her expertise"), we can lose if we haven't settled in our hearts to believe God and take Him at His word.

You and I can start today to stop this cycle in our lives. We can choose to stop being influenced by anything other than the Word of God. We can stop focusing on how big our problems are rather than how big our God is. Let's stop accepting less than what God provides.

NOTHING MORE, NOTHING LESS

When Jesus said, "It is finished," in John 19:30, He meant just that. Any blessing we ever need or desire from the Lord has already been given. God made the provision before we had the need. It's ours. Our needs are already met. Our healing is already done. Our deliverance is already done.

Are you sick and tired of what is going on in your life? Then get up from where you are and take the limits off. Take action like Jennifer Lopez in the movie *Enough*. She was tired of being abused by her crazy and selfish husband. She got up from her position of defeat and learned to fight, even if it meant death. She had enough. After all, what did she have to lose?

Have you had enough? Then stop limiting God. Allow God to do for you what you can't do for yourself. Don't put a lid on His power. He wants to show Himself strong on your behalf. Raise your expectation and expect Him to move in your life today.

There was a man who had been an invalid for 38 years. He sat at the pool near the Sheep Gate in Jerusalem waiting for an angel of the Lord to come and stir the water. The first one to go in after water was stirred was healed of his disease. It was enough to crush anyone's spirit and prompt a surrender to the circumstance. But one day, Jesus came by and asked him, "Do you want to get well?" I can almost visualize the man's expectation as he looked at Jesus with a sigh and said, "Yes, Lord," and maybe cried some tears. No limits. Jesus said, "Get up, take your bedroll, start walking." The man was healed on the spot. He picked up his bedroll and walked off (John 5:6-9). The man didn't argue with Jesus. It doesn't appear that he had thoughts of "I can't walk." He placed no limits.

Do you expect God to help you? Do you expect God to answer your prayer? Do you expect God to heal or deliver you? If you limit your expectations of God, you limit how He can work in your life. When we limit God, we are limiting ourselves. It's time for us to say "yes" and receive the promises of God. We need to possess our inheritance: joy, peace, healing, or whatever we may need. It's ours.

Look at what happened to King Asa. Instead of going to God the first time, he made a treaty with King Ben-Hadad, the King of Aram. The consequence was the army of the King of Aram escaping from King Asa's hand (2 Chronicles 16:7). That wasn't the case when he called on the Lord the next time when Zerah the Cushite with his thousands upon thousands came against Him. When Asa relied on Him, the Lord struck the Cushites before Asa and Judah (2 Chronicles 14:9-10, 12-14).

How often are we guilty of the same thing – leaning on others and not on God? God wants us to rely on Him and not place any limits. Nothing more. Nothing less. His power is the same today as it was yesterday (Hebrews 13:8). Allow Him to do it, whatever your "it" may be. No more limiting the One with whom all things are possible (Matthew 19:26) and with whom nothing is too hard (Genesis 18:14). No more leaning to our understanding and not depending on God.

Let's pray: *Lord, help us not to place a period where You've placed a comma. Help us to not limit You or Your power from doing a work in our lives. God, You have all power. When we forget, remind us of the cross and the price You paid. May we remember and not look at our circumstances, but rather to You with expectation. Amen.*

------------------**8**------------------

WILLING TO HAVE A
SUPPORTIVE TEAM

It's better to have a partner than go it alone.
Ecclesiastes 4:9 MSG

We've seen teams huddle before the game. The purpose is to bring the team together to strategize, motivate, or celebrate. Team members let each other know, "We got this," and then they play to win. The most confident of us tend to realize when we need to surrender to the support of a team.

Ecclesiastes 4:9-12 reminds us that two people are better than one person because they can enjoy a better benefit from their toil. It speaks of a cord of three strands not being quickly broken. The point is that if two are better than one, then how much better to have even more than two working together on our team?

From the moment the doctor said I had cancer, I knew the type of people I needed on my team. God prepared a team to come alongside me and lend their support. They had to be the type that weren't moved by what they heard, just like the ones I spoke to on the day the news was delivered. We teamed up to fight the good fight of faith and win.

Fred was out of town when my doctor first diagnosed me. My doctor said, "Linda, you need to call Fred and let him know." I initially refused. Can you imagine having to call someone miles away to say *I have cancer*?

"I'm not calling him to tell him that," I told the doctor, but after more prodding, I called Fred. "Fred, they're saying I have cancer."

He responded, "Well, tell them we ain't taking it." That's

what I needed to hear. That's the man I am so thankful God gave me to be on my team. After telling him, another team member rose to the occasion: my telephone rang as I was walking to another office the same day and it was my friend, Peggy. I told her what was going on and she responded, "The devil is a liar." Then, I overheard Jill, who joined me for the visit, saying to the ones in the room, "That's the kind of people she hangs around."

THE POWER OF TEAMWORK

From the beginning, it has never been God's design for us to handle everything on our own. We aren't meant to do life alone. In Genesis 2:18, God said, "It is not good for the man to be alone. I will make a helper suitable for him." So, he placed Adam into a coma and took one of his ribs. God made a woman from the rib he took out of Adam (Genesis 2:22). He blessed them and instructed them to be fruitful, multiply, and fill the earth. God had a plan. He knew Adam couldn't do it alone. He needed the participation and support of Eve. We would not be here if they had not teamed up and obeyed God (this time, anyway).

With any team, there must be some ground rules and some expectations. Many things have to be considered. What are the requirements to reach the goal? How does the team function? Can anyone be on it? You also have to *know* your team. Players need to know what's key to their positions (in other words, not everyone needs to know your business). Recognize that everyone isn't called to be on the team.

My team went into action once the decision was made to receive treatment in Birmingham. Everyone had a task. My daughter Shalunda's task was to find a place for us to live during that period. Would we stay at a hotel or find an apartment? She was to let us know how much money we needed. Fred was our designated driver and my backbone. My Mom was to tag along to keep her from staying at home worrying (LOL). Christi was to concentrate on her schooling.

When September 13, 2007, came, it was game time. It was time to see the specialist in Birmingham.

We did not find a place close to UAB's Kirklin Clinic. We made the decision to stay at the hotel, as needed, and travel back and forth from Dothan to Birmingham. The team - Fred, my Mom, Shalunda and of course, me - loaded in the vehicle like going on a family trip. Once there, we prepared ourselves for the one-and-a-half hour visit with the doctor. He was compassionate and very thorough. When he finished talking, I said, "I want you to be my doctor." The team chimed in agreement.

It was a good trip, but something happened on the way home. We had a team accident. A car in front of Fred abruptly stopped, causing a three-car collision. No one was injured except my Mom, who wasn't driving but hurt her foot. She's that front seat driver who tells you, "You're driving too close," "You're driving too fast" or "Watch out." She said she was mentally trying to help Fred put on the break when she physically hurt her foot. That's my mom.

There were more team trips to doctor visits. Most of them were just Fred and me. I have to say this: my Fred always treated me like a prized jewel and made me feel so special, even though I didn't share that feeling of myself because I didn't like the way I looked. Here I was all bald and wearing clothes that were too big for me due to weight loss. Instead of him commenting, we started a ritual where we would stop in Alabaster between the two cities to buy me a new outfit. He never complained and was so patient with me. I still do not have the words to describe Team Member Fred. I'm just grateful he qualified as my Man and was on my team.

TRYOUTS

You may not have as many members on your team as I did, but aim to always seek God on who should be on your team. Then, interview those team members. Ask them questions. You have every right. It's your team. Ask what they believe concerning

God and His promises. Have they been through any difficulties? How did they handle it? You need to know. It's just one way to weed out the team players from the bench warmers. I even asked my doctor plenty of questions to determine if he was an effective team member.

I'll say it again: everyone is not called or even qualified to be on your team. Do you think a coach would allow a 2-year-old to play on his professional team? Would you allow or even listen to someone teach a Bible study who doesn't believe in the Bible or the God of the Bible? As much as this resounds, "No," all day, it is the same concept with members of your team. This rule may include some well-meaning family members and friends. "Well-meaning" isn't good enough: King Asa removed his grandmother, Maacah, from being queen mother because she built a memorial to the whore goddess Asherah (1 Kings 15:13 MSG). This went against the team's goal.

Look how Jesus exemplified this when He went to Jairus' house:

He did not let anyone follow him except Peter, James and John the brother of James. When they came to the home of the synagogue leader, Jesus saw a commotion, with people crying and wailing loudly. He went in and said to them, "Why all this commotion and wailing? The child is not dead but asleep." But they laughed at him. After he put them all out, he took the child's father and mother and the disciples who were with him, and went in where the child was. Mark 5:37-42

Jesus "put them all out." The "all" was not on His team. You may have to do the same. Put them out! Your team need to know and support your goal. Make sure you have settled in your heart what you are aiming for prior to bringing people into your circle. My team's goal was to not be moved by what we heard. We were to believe the Word of God regardless of the circumstances. We were marching, in unison, to the beat of a different drummer (Jesus). Our Coach Jesus gave us the plan.

We were on the line ready to protect the quarterback (The Word in our hearts).

Chick-Fil-A is another example. They understand the concept of a team and the goal. It doesn't matter which location you visit; you will hear, "How may I help you?" "My pleasure," and "Thank you." The workers' posture is that of a supportive team working together with one common goal: to take care of the customer. We could learn some lessons from them.

Paul said to the Corinthians, "I appeal to you, brothers and sisters, in the name of our Lord Jesus Christ, that all of you agree with one another in what you say and that there be no divisions among you, but that you be perfectly united in mind and thought" (1 Corinthians 1:10).

Jesus knew the importance of being on one accord:

My prayer is not for them alone. I pray also for those who will believe in me through their message, that all of them may be one, Father, just as you are in me and I am in you. May they also be in us so that the world may believe that you have sent me. I have given them the glory that you gave me, that they may be one as we are one – I in them and you in me – so that they may be brought to complete unity. Then the world will know that you sent me and have loved them even as you have loved me.
John 17:20-23

There will be many voices attempting to speak into your life. Discern them because they're not all of God. You may not always be able to control what you hear but you get to decide how you respond. Turn a deaf ear when it's not of God.

MINDING THE TEAM'S BUSINESS

Our team must be single-minded, in harmony, in unity, and without dissent. A divided house cannot stand (Mark 3:25). A clear way to keep unity is by knowing that everyone doesn't need to know your business. Why should they? They have no need. Notice what happens the moment someone says, "I have cancer." People will tell you about their mother, uncle, cousin, or a friend that had the same thing, how bad it was on them, and that they died from it. Is that really what you want to hear? Ecclesiastes 3:7 reminds us that there is "...a time to be silent and a time to speak..." We have to learn those times.

Many, to include some family members, did not know that I was diagnosed with cancer. They could visibly see that I lost my hair and some weight, but no one dared ask me what was going on. It was like a hush matter. I mentioned this to my younger daughter, Christi, and she said, "Momma, it was not a topic for discussion."

There were some stares. A lady said, "I see you and I have the same problem."

I responded, "Oh, you had chemo?"

She responded, "No, no, I have alopecia!" I will never forget the look on her face.

Team business stays with the team. It should never be discussed outside the team. Don't feel obligated to share your business. That's why it's *your* business. Can you imagine Alabama telling Florida their football gameplays? Not hardly. If they aren't on your team, then they are bystanders. You see bystanders all the time and somehow, they seem to come out of the woodworks - like fleas. You see them looking out windows when they hear sirens, when a fight starts, a house is on fire, or even at the scene of an accident. They're standing around talking to everyone with their opinion. Leave them right there.

Bystanders were there when Jesus woke Lazarus (John 11:37). They said, "...Could not he who opened the eyes of the blind man have kept this man from dying?" Bystanders run their mouths without knowing the plan. Jesus said what He was going to do and did it. Can you imagine the opinions that must have flown left and right when Lazarus came out of the tomb: *Did you see that? It's sorcery, it's a trick, it's witchcraft, he wasn't really dead, I am out of here, or maybe He is who He says.* Some may have helped others from the ground who fainted seeing a dead man alive again. They were all bystanders – not team members. Again, leave them right there.

As I said earlier, Fred was out of town when the time came for my visit to the local oncologist, so my friend Jill went with me. The doctor told us that he was a general cancer doctor and was not familiar with non-Hodgkin's lymphoma. He recommended a bone marrow biopsy, CT/PET scan, and CHOP. The only chop I knew of was the ones I ate. "What is CHOP?" I asked him. I learned that CHOP is the acronym for a chemotherapy regimen used to treat patients with aggressive non-Hodgkin's lymphoma. Well, I wasn't feeling the CHOP. Looking intently at the doctor, I said, "I will do the scans and biopsy but you ain't going to CHOP me."

There was complete silence in the room for a couple of minutes. Jill knew it was time to interject. "Dr. Smith, may I ask you a question?" Jill asked. "You said you were not familiar with lymphoma. If this was someone you loved, what would you do?"

"I would send them to Birmingham," Dr. Smith replied. *Send someone he loved to Birmingham but treat me with CHOP*, I thought. The doctor and I looked at each other. Finally, he asked, "Would you like to go to Birmingham?"

I know I gave him one of my crazy looks. You know that look you give when someone said something and you're wondering, "Did he just say that?" Nevertheless, I responded, "Yeah," and I left there with a referral to Birmingham. I am grateful that Teammate Jill was there and knew the right questions to ask and when to hold me accountable.

I followed through on two of the doctor's recommended procedures prior to the Birmingham appointment. The bone marrow biopsy revealed no infiltration by lymphoma. The results of the CT/PET scan impression were: "Left cervical, adenopathy compatible with diagnosis of Hodgkin's Lymphoma. No distant metastasis. Otherwise negative." The doctor wrote:

I discussed with her the fact that the anaplastic large cell tumors carry, I believe, a slightly worse prognosis than most lymphomas and that probably the chance for us to cure this with simple CHOP chemotherapy here in Dothan is probably no more than 45-50% and she may end up needing a bone marrow transplant or more aggressive measures.... This was a very long and complicated meeting, we spent about two hours with the patient and a friend.

LET YOUR TEAM IN ON THE ACTION

We began to prepare ourselves for the trip to Birmingham. We didn't know what we would encounter or what we would do next. We had many questions and lots of uncertainties. We'd never been down this road before. We were traveling, in the dark, in a foreign land. The only comfort we had was that God was with us. Have you ever felt like that? Well, the stage was set.

As I spent days thinking about what direction to take, God used two ladies to speak to us as Fred and I were watching Trinity Broadcasting Network. Both described how God healed them of cancer but one lady went through chemo and the other did not. The one who had chemo didn't understand why she had to go through it to be healed. Fred and I looked at each other. We hadn't discussed the chemo aspect with anyone. These ladies answered a question we were pondering. Know that God can use anything – like a TV broadcast – or anyone to get His message delivered. He used a donkey to talk to Balaam in Numbers 22:28.

We continued to make preparations as we tried to process the unwelcomed detour in our lives. During this time, I kept feeling the urge to have another CT scan before the initial treatment. I couldn't shake it. I can't really say why I wanted another scan. Maybe it would show that the cancer was gone. It stayed on my mind. I spoke to Fred because this could result in another out-of-pocket expense for us. He supported me. I called the doctor and he authorized it. After all, the first scan didn't show any cancer. Maybe the new scan wouldn't show anything. The CT scan was performed on September 28, 2007. My abdomen, pelvis, and chest revealed no evidence of lymphoma, but the CT of my neck indicated multiple enlarged cervical lymph nodes consistent with a history of lymphoma.

Fred, my Mom, and I traveled to Birmingham, stayed at the hotel, and headed to the clinic the next day, October 1, 2007. I had an echocardiogram, lab work, and a visit planned with my doctor. I was loaded with questions: *Did you receive the bone marrow studies? What were the results of the CT scan from Friday? Has there been a change since the original diagnosis? If Chemo, would it shrink the tumor to normal? What about slow (mouth) release pills? You mentioned IV and tablets (what tablets)? If Chemo, what about other medicines – the effect – I may take: Hydrocodone (pain), Naprosyn, sinus infection medicine. If radiation, cumulative, symptoms, side effects? Any chance of contrast from CT scan causing a rash? Where's the Fish Place?* Okay, the last question had nothing to do with my purpose for seeing the doctor, but we heard about a place that had great fish.

Pause Break – Pause Break!

Let me encourage you to seek God and to be an active participant in your healthcare. Listen and ask questions. Research, Google (although some physicians frown on it), and at least be aware of what is going on in your situation. Sure, we may not be the schooled physician, but we are the ones on which they're practicing.

Back to the appointment. I knew I would be in the chemo treatment area the longest, so I armed myself with my praise and worship music and some headphones. I wanted to keep my spirit lifted so I wouldn't be moved by my surroundings. I had thoughts of how good the Lord was as my head and shoulders moved to the sound of the music. I was at peace. I finished treatment and off to the fish place we went. And yes, it was as good as we were told. We then headed back home.

STEPPING OUTSIDE THE PLAYBOOK

We aren't always on the mountaintop. Sometimes getting up or moving forward can be difficult. Trust me, I had my moments. Sometimes small gestures by teammates are what we need to walk with us through life's challenges.

One time my energy level was below zero and I wanted to get out of the house. This may seem simple, but it isn't when you are too weak to drive and the walls are closing in. I didn't ask my mom because she was caring for my sister. I called my aunt, Vivian, and she was busy. Everyone else was either at work or not available. My emotions were having a field day; they were up and down like a seesaw. I felt helpless. Then, my teammate, Elaine, called. Sensing something was wrong, she prayed against a spirit of depression. After praying, she said, "You need to get your butt out of the house. You get the new book that you ordered by Myles Munroe and go to the bookstore and read it."

I said, "Okay," and somehow forgot that I didn't have the energy to drive. Then the telephone rang. It was Vivian. She came over and I got out of the house like being released from prison.

There are times when you need more than a phone call or a ride and your team must be developed pretty quickly to help you achieve your goal. Here's an example: a couple was on a flight to Orlando to visit Disney World. The lady was almost seven months pregnant. Thirty minutes into the flight, she doubled over in pain and began bleeding. The flight attendants announced they needed a doctor, and an internist on the flight volunteered. The lady gave birth to a baby boy, but the umbilical cord was wrapped tightly around his neck so he wasn't breathing. Two paramedics rushed forward to help, one of whom specialized in infant respiratory procedures. He asked if anyone had a straw, which he wanted to use to suction fluid from the baby's lungs. The plane did not stock straws, but a flight attendant had a straw left over from a juice box she brought on board. The paramedic inserted the straw in the baby's lungs as the internist administered CPR. The internist asked for something he could use to tie off the umbilical cord. A passenger offered a shoelace. The baby whimpered and the crew announced that it was a boy. The parents gave the little boy the name Matthew. Matthew means "Godsent." Imagine if the lady was alone where no one could have come to her aid. She had a Godsent team working together for one common goal.

We see this in scripture as well. There was a team that wanted to get their friend, who could not walk, to Jesus to be healed (Mark 2:3-5). They couldn't get close to Him because of the crowd. In the natural, it looked like the odds were stacked against them, but they weren't deterred. There was no "It can't be done" or "There's no way." They made a hole through the roof. The team did what it took to achieve their goal to get to Jesus. Jesus saw their faith and their friend was healed. He always responds to faith.

WHEN TO TERMINATE

I received a letter from someone who wasn't on my team. He somehow found out about my decision to stop chemo treatment. There had been a breach on my team. Without notification, I figured it out and politely excused the member from my team. I'm sure she was concerned and feared the possibility of my death, but in a fight for my life, I could not carry the load of her fears. I needed strength.

There was another time I was approached by a busy-body. You know the type – always up in everybody's business. She had somehow heard of my decision. "They said you were stopping the chemo. You need to do what your doctor says," she said.

"I didn't ask your opinion," I replied.

"Well, I know you didn't but I'm still telling you. You need to do what your doctor says," she responded.

"Everyone has an opinion, like most people have buttholes, and this is my decision," I said. I know that last statement doesn't sound Christian-like, but it got her attention. Pray for me. I am still a work in progress and God isn't finished with me yet. I even told her, "You can take the other four treatments." She answered not a word and quietly left my office. Listen, we all have opinions and sometimes it pays to keep them to ourselves. The only opinion that matters is God's.

Let me make this disclaimer loud and clear so that there is no misunderstanding: **I AM NOT RECOMMENDING THAT ANYONE START OR STOP CHEMO TREATMENTS.** Everyone has to be persuaded in his or her own mind. You listen to the Lord and follow His leading. Following someone else could lead you to an early trip to the other side. I mean it. A young lady once told me, "You stopped chemo and I am too."

I responded, "And you're going to die. Don't ever do something because someone else did it. You need to hear the Lord for yourself." That young lady took my advice and lived because she sought the Lord. Have a conversation with the Lord. Follow His leading.

I have done my best to be the type of player that I would want on my team. My friend Joanne and I walked together in faith for some time. We loved our studies and enjoyed serving the Lord. We were like "two peas in a pod" on the same team. We loved going to garage (yard) sales, too. One day, she was confronted with some devastating news. She called me to the hospital to tell me the doctor said he had done all he could. We talked about what she would do and what she wanted me to do. Some difficult conversations and days followed but that's all part of being on a team. Joanne knew she could count on me. We traveled her journey until the end. We will be reunited one day where we are together with Jesus forevermore.

My oncologist referred me to a radiologist, Dr. Meredith, when I decided to stop chemo treatment. I followed up. I thought, "Here we go again on another journey down an untraveled road – Radiation Therapy." I felt comfortable with Dr. Meredith. I asked her, "What would you do if you were me?" She told me what she would do if she was in my situation. She explained everything in detail. Now, she did not tell me what to do. But because of the grace she used in our conversation and to everyone's surprise (including Fred and me), I agreed to receive the treatment. I asked and was referred to a local radiologist to complete the treatments. I had peace and felt good about my decision.

Before beginning radiation, I was fitted with a large face mask that would cover my head, neck, and shoulder area. I was secured to the XRT table to ensure there was no movement during treatment. They used a big machine that looked like a weapon from Star Wars. I can still hear those sounds as the machine would move around and then "boom" at the targeted neck areas. There is no way I could have done this alone. I had a well-qualified team with one goal in mind.

TAKING IN THE BLESSINGS OF A TEAM

Each year His Prison Ministries hosts a Christmas party for children of incarcerated parents. The youngest and smallest member of our team is my 5-year-old great-granddaughter, Brooklyn. We say what we're doing and she is on it: she will even encourage others to keep it moving. I've learned and have been encouraged by just being around and watching her. She is a team player.

I had the opportunity to lead a group about healing while attending a local church. I will forever be grateful for that opportunity as it caused me to stretch my faith and dig deeper into the Word. Our goal was to obtain what Jesus had purchased for us – our healing. We studied, researched, encouraged one another, and grew in our faith. We saw manifestations of the power of God. Our team played to win. Here's a story from my friend, Earl, whose life experienced the benefit of having a team:

For over a year, I had gone from doctor to doctor. One said "sinus infection" and another said "polyps." I was placed on antibiotics.

There was still no change. I started to have severe nose bleeds and was given an option of a higher dose of antibiotics or an MRI. I chose the MRI and that's when they found the tumor. It was Nasopharyngeal cancer and malignant neoplasm of the bones of the skull and face. My wife, Michelle, and I were floored. We had no insurance and were right in the middle of adopting our granddaughter who was less than a year old. We cried and cried. It dawned on me, "I ain't ready to die." I was scared.

My ENT referred me to a local doctor who said he would try to get me seen in Birmingham under their charity program. Michelle took the initiative and started calling Birmingham and within a week or two we were seen. The charity program wasn't available at the time so we came back home to see what could be done in the meantime. I had to get all of my top teeth pulled to start radiation due to the location of the cancer. Swollen from my tooth removal while trying to figure out what to do because we had no insurance, we met with the local oncologist. He never came up to me to ask how I was feeling or what was going on. He told me I was scheduled to have surgery the next morning and that chemo would be placed in my side. He said I would do chemo for two straight weeks. Michelle asked him where he was coming up with this information. He said he never had a case like this and had pulled the information off the internet. Michelle said, "We may not have insurance but my husband isn't going to be treated like a lab rat." Michelle called the doctor in Birmingham and sent a copy of what the doctor had printed off the internet. The doctor said, "No," and "if you had done this therapy, you would have died." I wouldn't be here if Michelle hadn't got on it.

I started radiation treatment. I was locked down in my mask on the table. I could hear the technician talking to someone outside the treatment area while I was struggling to breathe. The tumor blocked my airway. I managed to get my hands free so I could get up. I left and never went back. The charity program eventually became available in Birmingham. There was a group of 10 doctors studying my case because it was rare. I was told that within a month, I would lose my eyesight and memory. That never happened. I was given three to four months to live and sent home to make funeral plans. While making funeral arrangements, the lady who worked there invited me

to her church, told us about their Healing Class, and introduced us to Linda. I received prayer and started attending the healing classes.
We went back to Birmingham. Before I did my first chemo, they did another scan. The tumor was gone. The doctors couldn't believe it. They were in total awe. We told them we had a lot of people praying. Michelle told them she had been praying, too. One of the doctors said, "I don't believe in miracles."
Although it was gone, they said they wanted to take precautions and continue with their plan of care because of where it was and that it could come back. Michelle had to stop work and we stayed in Birmingham for six months. I had radiation treatment Monday through Friday and chemo once a week. Another scan was done after the second or third chemo treatment and still no tumor. And the doctors were still in awe.
I want to say this: Do not quit moving when they say you got "whatever." If you stop, it's going to jump on you. I walked. I kept going. I am here today because of prayer. We couldn't have gone through this by ourselves.
Michelle said, "It shook me but then I got more faith. I prayed – not just prayed – I asked God to please heal my husband. We couldn't have gone through this by ourselves."

God had a team in place for Earl and He has one for you, too. In the Bible, there was a group of people who decided to build a city with a tower that would reach to heaven. Their goal was to make a name for themselves and stay together. The Lord saw the city and tower they were building (Genesis 11:1-7). The Lord said, "If as one people speaking the same language, they have begun to do this, then nothing they plan to do will be impossible for them" (verse 6). They were a team – one people with one language. God recognized that nothing they planned to do would be impossible for them.

The perfect example of a team and how it functions is found in the Godhead: Father, Son, and Holy Spirit. A team with one goal, on one accord: to redeem the fallen man.

There was a team who prayed for me as I wrote this book. We're in a Small Group together. I was having some difficulty finishing my book and asked for prayer during our meeting. The next day I received a text from my sister, who knew nothing of the ladies praying for me. She said she saw me in a dream and a lady interceding in prayer for me. I finished writing the book within the week. I know it was the result of the team praying for me.

Pause Break – Pause Break!

Who's on your team? Do they meet the qualifications? Are there members on your team who should not be? If yes, then dismiss them. It's your team and you don't need any bystanders. Do they know the goal? Does your team operate as one people with one language to meet the goal? Do they know how to fight the good fight of faith to win?

Is Jesus on your team? If not, you may want to consider asking Him to join. You will find Him to be your most valuable member. He knows all the plays.

----------------9----------------

WILLING TO HAVE PEACE

Peace I leave with you, my peace I give unto you: not as the world giveth, give I unto you. Let not your heart be troubled, neither let it be afraid. John 14:27 KJV

Jesus said, "…in Me you may have [perfect] peace. In the world you have tribulation and distress and suffering, but be courageous [be confident, be undaunted, be filled with joy]; I have overcome the world…." (John 16:33 AMP).

This sounds great, doesn't it? But let's be honest. Peace is not among our first thoughts when the pressure is on. How can we have peace when life keeps shifting? Where is peace when you've lost your job and can't provide for your family? Where is peace when it seems like all hell has broken loose? How can you have peace when you've been told, "You have three to four months to live. Go home and make arrangements." Other things, in addition to the thought, *I am going to die*, race through your mind, and peace is not one of them.

At the time I'm writing this book, we are in the middle of a coronavirus pandemic. The norm, whatever it may have been, is no longer. This virus has affected the country – the entire world, actually – and stress levels are up. People are anxious and unsure of what to believe with all the different reports from the White House to the outhouse.

Yet, God has given us a promise of perfect peace in the midst of all we experience. The biblical concept of peace means to be complete or to be sound, or to live well. The race will continue until we believe the Word and obtain God's peace. Once we get it, we have to walk it out.

PEACE FROM A BIBLICAL PERSPECTIVE

There is no promise in the Bible that says we will experience freedom from worry, trouble, trial, temptation, loss, or disappointments. On the contrary, we are told these things will come. But the peace of God in the midst of our challenges is not as the world sees peace.

Imagine being with Jesus when He said, "I am leaving this world and going back to my Father." This wasn't what His disciples expected to hear. They were upset. Jesus consoled them:

Peace I leave with you; My [perfect] peace I give to you; not as the world gives do I give to you. Do not let your heart be troubled, nor let it be afraid. [Let My perfect peace calm you in every circumstance and give you courage and strength for every challenge.]
John 14:27 AMP

The world sees peace as the absence of tumult, violence, or persecution. God's peace is a peace of mind and heart. It transcends all understanding, meaning we can't comprehend the fullness of true peace because it's not something that can be created. God's peace is constant. It is not dependent on what is going on in the world. The peace of the Lord is a gift to those who submit their will to Him that He may do His work through them. It can never be experienced outside of God.

We have a sense of peace with our alarm systems, insurance, and retirement accounts. But in the end, these things cannot provide true security or true peace. The stock market crashes, the locks have to be replaced, and the alarm system stops working without batteries. All of our manmade elements of peace can fail. So, why would we settle for worldly peace when it is all circumstantial?

We experience true peace as we place our issues under the light of God's Word. God's Word is light and we can have peace in that light. This kind of peace is not linked to any external circumstances. It comes from knowing Jesus.

Isaiah 26:1-2 speaks of a "perfect peace" and compares it to a city with walls and bulwarks, which are symbols of security. Only those who trust in the Lord and "keepeth the truth" may enjoy the perfect peace (KJV). We do so under one condition:

You will keep in perfect peace those whose minds are steadfast, because they trust in you.
Isaiah 26:3

Pause Break – Pause Break!

God is offering you His peace, free of charge. Do you know of a god that offers perfect peace in the midst of our trials and uncertainties? Why not trade in your worries? It's a great exchange for peace.

Our minds must be steadfast in order to trust the Source of Peace. In fact, perfect peace is the Lord Himself within us. Our minds lean on and trust in Him. Our mind is "perfect" or imperfect to the degree that our "mind is stayed on" God rather than our circumstances. Do you want peace? Then, remain in Him. Does this not make you long for His perfect peace?

EVEN WHEN IT DOESN'T ADD UP

Again, peace is not the absence of trouble. The psalmist said:

He will not fear bad news; His heart is steadfast, trusting [confidently relying on and believing] in the Lord. His heart is upheld, he will not fear While he looks [with satisfaction] on his adversaries.
Psalm 112:7-8 AMP

The psalm tells us the psalmist does not fear bad news, which tells us that bad news, indeed, will come. We don't have to fear bad news, either.

I've spoken to several people who have gone through some major life issues. They spoke of having God's peace. They said, "I can't explain it, but I wasn't worried. Everyone around me was. I was at peace."

I, too, was at peace when the Lord spoke to me about my situation. I can't explain it, either, but I knew I couldn't be moved by the circumstances because my external circumstances didn't look good at all. I stopped chemo treatment knowing death could happen. Or at least, that's what I was told. But I had an inner peace. Inner peace is our entire being – our heart – at rest. Circumstances are temporary and God is sovereign over all.

Remember the former things, those of long ago; I am God, and there is no other; I am God, and there is none like me. I make known the end from the beginning, from ancient times, what is still to come. I say, 'My purpose will stand, and I will do all that I please.' From the east I summon a bird of prey; from a far-off land, a man to fulfill my purpose. What I have said, that I will bring about; what I have planned, that I will do.
Isaiah 46:9–11

Every day brings new challenges to our peace. But every day also holds a new promise of peace. Horatio Gates Spafford (1828-1888) placed his trust in God during his life's prosperity, but also during its calamities. He and his wife had four daughters and one son. He was a successful attorney and real estate broker. Then, things changed. He lost a fortune in the Great Chicago Fire. At about the same time, he lost his 4-year-old son to scarlet fever. A few years later in 1873, Horatio sent his wife and daughters on a boat trip to Europe with plans to join them after finishing some business in Chicago. A few days later, he received a telegram from his wife that the ship wrecked and all four of his daughters were dead. He passed over the same sea where his daughters died to meet his wife. It was then that he wrote the hymn, "It Is Well With My

Soul[39]." How could his soul be "well" with such a loss? It was his faith and trust in the Lord that gave him peace. What a testimony.

We can have peace during challenges when we remember "...that in all things God works for the good of those who love him, who have been called according to his purpose" (Romans 8:28).

HOW TO SEE WHAT WE'RE GOING THROUGH

It is important to remember that there is purpose in our trials. If you're a believer, God can bring good things from our afflictions (again, Romans 8:28). Even the discipline and chastening of the Lord will "yield the peaceable fruit of righteousness" in our lives (Hebrews 12:11). Challenges provide an opportunity for "hoping in God" and eventually "praising Him" (Psalm 43:5). They help us "comfort" others when they undergo similar trials (2 Corinthians 1:4), and they "achieve for us an eternal glory that far outweighs them all" (2 Corinthians 4:17).

Imagine helping someone overcome a struggle by encouraging them to not give up and trust the Lord. Imagine watching their lives change for the better because you offered them hope. People are hurting. They need to know that there is a God who loves and cares for them and can bring them through life challenges.

I noticed a young man hanging around a gas station one day. I greeted him. As we continued to talk, I learned that he was homeless. He told me he had just thought about giving up that day and had nothing to live for. I told him about his value and that our meeting was not by accident. I believe he received some peace as we continued to talk. When we finished, he said, "Can I give you a hug?"

I said, "Well, they say not to with this COVID going on but

---

[39] Discipleship Ministries: History of Hymns: It is Well with My Soul, 2013

what the heck." We hugged.
Be encouraged by Zakiya as she shares her testimony:

In 1998 I was diagnosed with breast cancer. I told no one. I mean no one, not even my mom or any of my family or best friends. This will be a first for a lot to hear of it. I was raised in such a way that you didn't discuss your personal business, so I didn't. I went through chemo all alone. People couldn't figure out why I was spiraling out of control, wilding out, becoming an alcoholic, clubbing, dropping out of college, and having this 'I don't care' attitude. I was a mother but I figured since I had what most consider a death sentence, I'd let my mom raise my son (that was her baby anyway at the time). I figured I'd go out with a bang.

Fast forward to Oct. 2000 when I rung the bell for being Cancer-free for now 20 years. Though these years have definitely been an uphill battle, and I've had my share of roller coaster rides, I'm still here. One thing I know to be true is it's not what THEY say; it's what HE says. So, for the ones fighting battles and illnesses that no one has any clue about, DON'T GIVE UP and know you're not alone. We all have to go one day but if you're able to still write your story, then do it. I asked all the questions to include, "Why me?" I almost gave up. Then, I heard this voice that said "LIVE" and that's what I've tried to do. I'm not perfect. I still have my down days. I sometimes hurt. I wear myself thin a lot of times. But for me, when it's time to REST it'll be FINAL! So LIVE, LOVE, LAUGH.

A relationship with God allows us to keep things in proper perspective as we choose peace rather than give way to fear and worry. Even now, I walk in peace knowing that the last report I was given from a doctor included a 30% survival rate. You can live at peace, too, regardless of what it looks like or what you've been told. Just trust the One who gave you His word. Our lives are in His hands. We will not leave this world until our appointed time, which only He knows.

If it happens to be our appointed time, we just need to make sure our house is in order so we can stand before Him. Our house isn't referring to where we live as much as it is our actual being. We have nothing to lose because we will be in His presence forevermore when we get to heaven – if we believe in the Lord Jesus Christ while we are here on earth. There are no more challenges, trouble, disappointments, anxiety, sickness, or pain in Heaven. We'll have joy forevermore.

PRAY FOR PEACE

As humans, we get tired of the constant struggles. Jesus tells us, "Come to me, all you who are weary and burdened, and I will give you rest. Take my yoke upon you and learn from me, for I am gentle and humble in heart, and you will find rest for your souls. For my yoke is easy and my burden is light" (Matthew 11:28-30). He promises rest for our souls. No worries, but rest. But we must do our part: come to Him, take his yoke, and learn from Him. We only learn as we spend time with Him in study. Peace comes from a saving knowledge of Jesus.

As we spend more time with Him, we learn that we can experience peace as a result of prayer. Philippians 4:6-7 (AMP) says:

Do not be anxious or worried about anything, but in everything [every circumstance and situation] by prayer and petition with thanksgiving, continue to make your [specific] requests known to God. And the peace of God [that peace which reassures the heart, that peace] which transcends all understanding, [that peace which] stands guard over your hearts and your minds in Christ Jesus [is yours].

Anxiety weighs the heart down and can cause depression (Proverbs 12:25). God gives us a way out. We don't have to be anxious or worry about anything. We don't even have to worry about tomorrow: what we will eat, drink, or what we will put on (Matthew6:25-34). Oh, how He loves us! Who wouldn't want to serve a God like ours?

Over and over again, we see in the Word where people prayed and God worked on their behalf. Remember the word to Jehoshaphat: "You will not have to fight this battle. Take up your positions; stand firm and see the deliverance the Lord will give you, Judah and Jerusalem. Do not be afraid; do not be discouraged. Go out to face them tomorrow, and the Lord will be with you[41]." The people just had to stand still and see the deliverance of God. He even revealed their enemies' plans.

We have a friend in Jesus. We can take everything to Him in prayer and find help in our time of need and peace. I prayed while going from doctor to doctor, "Lord, I am going to the doctor. I don't know what's going on. None of them know either."

Then the Lord said, "Lymphoma. Don't be moved by what you hear." Peace replaced my anxiety. Oh, thank you, Lord!

If King Hezekiah was here, I believe he would tell you to trust and rely confidently on the Lord. He would tell you about the time of his anxiety when the King of Assyria (Sennacherib) came up against Him. Sennacherib tried discouraging King Hezekiah's people:

Thus says the king, "Do not let Hezekiah deceive you, for he will not be able to rescue you from my hand; nor let Hezekiah make you trust in and rely on the Lord, saying, 'The Lord will certainly rescue us, and this city [of Jerusalem] will not be given into the hand of the king of Assyria.' Do not listen to Hezekiah, for thus says the king of Assyria: 'Surrender to me and come out to [meet] me, and every man may eat from his own vine and fig tree, and every man may drink the waters of his own well, until I come and take you away to a land like your own land, a land of grain and new wine, a land of bread and vineyards, a land of olive trees and honey, so that you may live and not die.' Do not listen to Hezekiah when he misleads and incites you, saying, 'The Lord will rescue us!'"
2 Kings 18:29-32 AMP

King Hezekiah heard what was said and went into the temple of the Lord. He sent word to the prophet, Isaiah:

---

[41] 2 Chronicles 20:17

"This is a day of distress and anxiety, of punishment and humiliation;
for children have come to [the time of their] birth and there is no
strength to rescue them. It may be that the Lord your God will hear
all the words of the Rabshakeh, whom his master the king of Assyria
has sent to taunt and defy the living God, and will rebuke the words
which the Lord your God has heard. So offer a prayer for the remnant
[of His people] that is left [in Judah]." So the servants of King
Hezekiah came to Isaiah. Isaiah said to them, "Say this to your
master: 'Thus says the Lord, "Do not be afraid because of the words
that you have heard, ...
2 Kings19:3-6 AMP

The Lord said, "Do not be afraid because of the words that you
have heard." Surely God knew Sennacherib's reputation. But
yet, He sent word to not be afraid. You would think it should
have ended there, but Sennacherib sent another message
challenging Hezekiah's faith (2 Kings 19:10-13). God answered
again.

Then Isaiah the son of Amoz sent word to Hezekiah, saying, "Thus
says the Lord, the God of Israel: 'I have heard your prayer to Me
regarding Sennacherib king of Assyria.' This is the word that
the Lord has spoken against him: 'Therefore thus says
the Lord concerning the king of Assyria: "He will not come to this city
[Jerusalem] nor shoot an arrow there; nor will he come before it with
a shield nor throw up a siege ramp against it. By the way that he
came, by the same way he will return, and he will not come into this
city,"' declares the Lord. 'For I will protect this city to save it, for My
own sake and for My servant David's sake.'"
2 Kings 19:20-34 AMP

It happened as the Lord said. Sennacherib never stepped foot
into the city. He was killed by his sons while he was
worshipping his god. This is what happens when we have

a relationship with the Lord, cast our cares on him, take Him at His Word, and walk in faith. We win! God is no respecter of persons. He did it for King Hezekiah and He will do it for us.

FIGHT PAST BEING AFRAID

As we seek to find peace in our lives, understand that fear will try to creep in. But fear and peace cannot co-exist. It's too much like split personalities. Fear paralyzes. The enemy uses it to try and steal our hope. It's an ongoing fight. The only way to win is by trusting God. The Lord is on our side and we don't have to fear (Psalm 118:6).

Even when trusting God, we may still have some apprehensions. But do whatever He says despite them. Do it afraid. You have nothing to lose. We push ourselves and go to work when we don't feel like it, don't we? We know if we don't show up, we won't get a paycheck. Well, there's a spiritual paycheck waiting for us. It's called "Peace." Just like King David, we can put our trust and faith in God when we are afraid (Psalm 56:3 AMP). Here's some more comforting news: we aren't the first to experience fear and we won't be the last. Let me tell you about Gideon (Judges 7-8:21). God sent an angel to speak to Gideon while he was gathering wheat. Israel was surrounded by the army of the Midianites and cut off from supplies. Gideon was working diligently when he got the message that God wanted him to lead an army against the enemy. Gideon wanted a sign (Judges 6:17). He was afraid when he realized it was the angel of the Lord, but the angel reminded him to have peace and not to be afraid because he was not going to die.

Gideon prepared to follow God's command and gathered all the men he could to go against Midian. His army numbered 32,000 men. But God said that was too many. All those who were afraid – 22,000 – were released to go back home. God said that the 10,000 left were still too many (Judges 7:3). Gideon was left with 300 men.

It's time to drop the mic: Gideon went from 32,000 to 300 men! Imagine standing against a 135,000-men army of the Midianites. This is scary. However, God told Gideon He was going to give the Midianites into his hand. It may not have made sense, but Gideon decided to trust God and stand in peace. With trumpets, clay pots and lanterns in hand, the men broke their pots and blew their horns at Gideon's signal. The men of Midian were startled awake with all the noise. Confused, they began fighting one another (Judges 8:10-12). God gave the 300-men army of Israel victory over the 135,000-men army of Midian! I gave you the short version. Go read the whole story. It's encouraging.

Even Jesus' disciples experienced being afraid. Remember Peter's story (look back in Chapter 6). Peter had peace walking on the water because Jesus said, "Come." Peter didn't begin to sink until he saw the wind. He forgot Jesus and took his eyes off of him. Fear crept in. Let this be a reminder for us to keep our eyes on Jesus. Stop looking around, or sink.

Jesus is still saying, "Come." We can have peace while walking on the water of our circumstances as we keep our eyes on Him. We are not to be moved by what we see or hear. We don't have to be afraid. We just need to listen and trust in Him.

I will listen to what God the Lord says; he promises peace to his people, his faithful servants ...
Psalm 85:8

Finding peace requires standing firm while trusting God. How? We set the atmosphere by inviting Him in. Keep the Word before your eyes: study, put on some praise and worship music, pray and just enjoy His presence. Be obedient and do whatever He says. God told the Israelites:

If you follow my decrees and are careful to obey my commands, I will send you rain in its season, and the ground will yield its crops and the trees their fruit. Your threshing will continue until grape harvest and the grape harvest will continue until planting, and you will eat all

the food you want and live in safety in your land. I will grant peace in the land, and you will lie down and no one will make you afraid. I will remove wild beasts from the land, and the sword will not pass through your country.
Leviticus 26:3-6

You can get God's peace right now. Here are some scriptures to declare:

I will both lay me down in peace, and sleep: for thou, Lord, only makest me dwell in safety.
Psalm 4:8 KJV

Great peace have they which love thy law: and nothing shall offend them.
Psalm 119:165 KJV

For I know the plans I have for you," declares the Lord, "plans to prosper you and not to harm you, plans to give you hope and a future.
Jeremiah 29:11

Don't be moved by your senses and allow them to threaten your peace. If you do, then peace – based on a feeling or the absence of something else – will be "gone like the wind." You see, peace can't sustain itself. We only have to look around and see the disintegration of peace in marriages, in families, among friends, and nations. It's a vicious cycle. These things will continue until Jesus returns to establish lasting peace. But even so, we can have His peace through it all. Remember what He said:

Peace I leave with you; My [perfect] peace I give to you; not as the world gives do I give to you. Do not let your heart be troubled, nor let it be afraid. [Let My perfect peace calm you in every circumstance and give you courage and strength for every challenge.]
John 14:27 AMP

We don't have to be worried, concerned, uneasy, apprehensive, fearful, perturbed, troubled, bothered, disturbed, distressed, fretful, agitated, nervous, antsy, tense, uptight, or jittery. These are ingredients for high blood pressure, a heart attack, stroke, or death. God's peace is much better. The world can't give us the peace of God. Only Jesus can. We can have His perfect peace – the peace of God which surpasses all understanding (Philippians 4:7).

Take your stand. Stay determined to seek and experience God's peace.

WILLING TO STAND

"…and having done all, to stand." Ephesians 6:13

Life often feels like a cycle of conflict. We finish one battle and then comes another one. Is there any rest for the weary? As if issues from COVID-19 aren't enough, we find ourselves involved in racial and political issues. Do we get a break?

Paul understood the battles. He said:

We are pressured in every way [hedged in], but not crushed; perplexed [unsure of finding a way out], but not driven to despair; hunted down and persecuted, but not deserted [to stand alone]; struck down, but never destroyed; always carrying around in the body the dying of Jesus, so that the [resurrection] life of Jesus also may be shown in our body. For we who live are constantly [experiencing the threat of] being handed over to death for Jesus' sake, so that the [resurrection] life of Jesus also may be evidenced in our mortal body [which is subject to death]. So physical death is [actively] at work in us, but [spiritual] life [is actively at work] in you.
2 Corinthians 4:8-12 AMP

Our very lives and future are on the line. Is there any hope? What can we do? Paul gives the answers in Ephesians 6. We arm ourselves by putting on the full armor of God and then we stand. Ephesians 6:10-12 says:

And that about wraps it up. God is strong, and he wants you strong. So take everything the Master has set out for you, well-made weapons of the best materials. And put them to use so you will be able to stand up to everything the Devil throws your way. This is no afternoon athletic contest that we'll walk away from and forget about in a couple of hours. This is for keeps, a life-or-death fight to the finish against the Devil and all his angels. (MSG)

Here's another version of the same scripture:

In conclusion, be strong in the Lord [draw your strength from Him and be empowered through your union with Him] and in the power of His [boundless] might. Put on the full armor of God [for His precepts are like the splendid armor of a heavily-armed soldier], so that you may be able to [successfully] stand up against all the schemes and the strategies and the deceits of the devil. For our struggle is not against flesh and blood [contending only with physical opponents], but against the rulers, against the powers, against the world forces of this [present] darkness, against the spiritual forces of wickedness in the heavenly (supernatural) places. (AMP)

The armor is for use in a spiritual battle because our fight is not against other people. Our fight is with the spirits behind the diagnoses, the circumstances, the arguments, and trials in which we find ourselves. Our all-knowing God knew we couldn't handle the fight against these principalities alone. So, He provided us with ammunition to counter the enemy's attacks.

Be prepared. You're up against far more than you can handle on your own. Take all the help you can get, every weapon God has issued, so that when it's all over but the shouting you'll still be on your feet. Truth, righteousness, peace, faith, and salvation are more than words. Learn how to apply them. You'll need them throughout your life. God's Word is an indispensable weapon. In the same way, prayer is essential in this ongoing warfare. Pray hard and long. Pray for your brothers and sisters. Keep your eyes open. Keep each other's spirits up so that no one falls behind or drops out.
Ephesians 6: 13-18 MSG

Let's take a closer look at the armor we are to put on.

BELT OF TRUTH The belt of truth is the first item in our arsenal. Every other piece of the armor is attached to the belt of truth. If you don't begin with truth, you'll never defeat the enemy. A belt holds the other pieces of clothing and armor together. It secures the outfit and allows a soldier to move freely. Truth both secures us and gives us freedom. What is the truth? The truth is the Word of God (John 17:17). With the belt of truth around our waists, we are prepared to stand against the lies of the enemy.

BREASTPLATE OF RIGHTEOUSNESS Righteousness means "being made right." The breastplate of righteousness covers our hearts and other vital organs. In a sense, the breastplate covers the most vulnerable areas of a warrior. Proverbs 4:23 says, "Above all else, guard your heart, for everything you do flows from it." We need the complete righteousness of God provided in Christ (2 Corinthians 5:21).

FOOTWEAR OF THE READINESS OF THE GOSPEL Our feet are to be fitted with the readiness that comes from the gospel of peace. The gospel is the good news. Ephesians repeatedly reminds us to "stand" and "stand firm." One of the easiest ways for the enemy to succeed in shaking us loose from standing firm is to tempt us to worry. When we carry anxiety and worry, we are robbed of peace. The gospel of peace keeps our feet anchored and standing firm.

SHIELD OF FAITH The shield of faith is used to "extinguish all the flaming darts of the evil one." Roman soldiers carried shields that were covered with heavy animal hide. Before a battle, they would dip their shields into the water so that when fiery darts hit them, the wet hide extinguished the darts. When Satan attacks us, our faith in God lessens the blow because we've been "dipped" into the water of God's word. We can withstand the attack because we know in whom we believe.

HELMET OF SALVATION A helmet protects the brain, or basically our minds. The battlefield of our mind is the primary place the spiritual battle is fought. The Lord works His truth into our perspectives while the enemy fights for strongholds to bind us (John 10:10). Our minds are protected because of Jesus' work on the cross; we have been given the mind of Christ. A helmet can also serve as a signifier. When the enemy looks at us, he sees that we belong to Jesus.

SWORD OF THE SPIRIT The sword of the Spirit is the Word of God. The sword is the one offensive weapon on the list. Hebrews 4:12 says, "For the word of God is alive and active. Sharper than any double-edged sword, it penetrates even to dividing soul and spirit, joints and marrow; it judges the thoughts and attitudes of the heart." Second Timothy 3:16 speaks of Scripture as being "God-breathed." When God spoke, creation came into existence. He breathed life into man. There is power in the Word of God. This is why it is our best offense.

PRAYER Prayer is essential to using the armor of God. Prayer is the way we draw strength from God and rely on Him. First Thessalonians 5:17 tells us to "pray without ceasing." See more on this in the chapter, "Willing to Pray."

God prepared His armor so we could be strong and stand, and not just for a season. He wants us to stand until we finish our race. Take the time to research and get an in-depth understanding of God's armor. After all, you will be wearing it. And, again, there's just something special about seeking for yourself with the help of the Holy Spirit.

WALK BY FAITH

There is power in your testimony. Once you've stood with the armor of God, go ahead and start giving your testimony. Don't wait for the final diagnosis or the manifestation. Start walking by faith. Call those things that are not as though they were. Revelation 12:11 says, "They triumphed over him by the blood of the Lamb and by the word of their testimony; they did not love their lives so much as to shrink from death." Their testimony was a part of their victory. They stuck to the truth and declared their belief in it. They did not shrink back when threatened with death, but remained firm (they took a stand). They were not afraid to die if it came down to death. They left their dying testimony to the truth and power of God.

The enemy's time is running out and he's angry because we're standing. He sees we're willing to die for what and in whom we believe. Your testimony matters.

How can we testify when the things we desire have not happened? We do so when we continue to walk by faith and not by sight. Faith operates in the unseen by testifying that we are trusting and believing in our all-powerful God. I took a stand and God consistently demonstrated His power throughout my journey. There is no way, on my own, that I could have exhibited what the doctors documented:

September 13, 2007   On examination, she was a cheerful well-appearing 51-year-old woman who looked younger than her stated age.... She was alert and appropriate, remarkably calm, and appeared well.

October 1, 2007 On examination, she was calm and well.

October 24, 2007 On examination, she was cheerful and well.

January 16, 2008 On examination, she was well.

March 31, 2008 On examination, she was calm. She appeared well.

September 3, 2008 On examination, she was cheerful; she looked very well. She was very well.

January 21, 2009 On examination, cheerful, very well, with a marked residual alopecia. Cheerful and very well.

April 15, 2009 Ms. Wimes is here for a routine follow up visit today. She feels extremely well.

July 21, 2009 On examination, she was in very good spirits and appeared well. She appeared well and in good spirits.

October 29, 2009 On examination, cheerful, well, good spirits. She was alert and appropriate and in good spirits. She did not exhibit signs of anxiety or depression.
January 25, 2010 On examination, cheerful, well-appearing. She was in good spirits and appeared well.
July 19, 2010 On examination, cheerful, well. She was cheerful, well, appropriate and did not exhibit signs of anxiety or depression.
November 15, 2010 At the time of the patient's visit, she felt well.

Did you read the number of times the doctors said, "Well"? By the end of it all they were saying it as often as I was. Look at God!

Go ahead and give your testimony. Others need to hear it. Our testimony is our secret weapon, and this is one secret we don't need to keep – even if it's not our own testimony. I met a young mother named Kim. I soon learned she was battling breast cancer among other things. I did not know about breast cancer but I knew God had healed Dot of throat cancer. I just figured He could handle breast cancer, too. I told Kim about Dot and she was encouraged. We became friends and I remained a part of her team.

Another young lady, LaKeiya, wants to share her testimony about being healed of colon cancer:

I was diagnosed with Stage 3 Colon Cancer in January 2011. I had surgery and received six months of chemotherapy. This ordeal changed my world. I felt helpless and depressed. Different, well-meaning people were telling me what and what not to do. Then Pastor Brian told me to call Ms. Linda because she had been through cancer. I didn't want to call another person and hear them tell me what to do. I figured she was like the others. I called and found her to be everything Pastor Brian said: down to earth. She encouraged me and was a God-sent. She shared her experience and walked through this time with me. She helped me to realize that I had to depend on and trust the Lord. I relied on my faith and the Word of God. I put into practice what she shared. I only allowed positive people around me. My team was very limited. I would not be here today if it wasn't for God's grace. God is real and I am a living witness that He still heals. I share my testimony of what the Lord did for me to help others, to include a family member battling Stage 4 Colon Cancer.

We all have a testimony. It may seem like nothing to you, but understand what *you* consider nothing or even insignificant may touch and give hope to someone in a crisis or someone who is about to give up. I am reminded of a soldier who came to me about a matter. Both he and his wife were dealing with some issues. I later felt compelled to share my testimony and sent his wife an email, not knowing what the result would be. Here's a portion of her response:

I wanted to take the opportunity to personally thank you for your lovely e-mail and for the warmth of your concern and prayers. I, too, am a believer and I truly believe through GOD our Lord and Savior all things are possible. I must confess that I have called upon Him many times as the great Physician and Healer to heal those who are experiencing illness, pain or sorrow. I am quick to tell people, "Do not own what God hasn't given you" and that doctors are merely men and women who are "practicing" medicine. It is through the guidance of our Lord and Savior that they can make a difference. Yet, as I watched my physician utter the words "complex mass" and probable renal cancer, all alone, I found it difficult to ask the Lord to carry me through the very things I do for others. It was through the grace of people such as yourself that I was covered in prayer and that prayer has seen me through what appeared to be a downhill spiral. It has been a rough (3) months; as someone who kept up with routine assessments, I found myself wading through unfamiliar territory. While my back injury is what landed me in the hospital, it soon became apparent it would be the least of our concerns. I felt "guilty" about asking the Lord to help me, like I was laying another burden at his feet. Believe me when I say, I felt the warmth of your prayers and the movement of His power. While I was waiting on additional tests and CT results, more issues popped up in other areas, yet I felt a peace. Others around me were racked with worry, yet I had a calmness. I could feel the power of the prayers and I knew that God would not forsake me. It freed me to be able to ask GOD to cover me as well, and through his grace our prayers were answered. So, PRAISE BE TO GOD, the tumor has not grown in the last (60) days... The second surgery on my back revealed no cancer in the area around the lesion removal and the ovarian issues have resolved as well. I am a walking testimony to the Power of Prayer. Offering you a simple "thank you" seems so understated for all you and your friends have done for me and my family. I believe everyone enters our lives for a reason and I am thankful that you had the opportunity to meet my husband and to touch our lives so deeply! We were truly blessed with the introduction of you into our lives and for that we will be eternally grateful.

Being obedient in sharing your testimony pays off. Someone could be delivered and set free. The enemy doesn't want us to share it. That's a good reason to do it. You never know who needs to be encouraged. Do what God says. Not only will we be blessed, but God gets the glory. Just one word – your testimony – could encourage someone to stand and trust God.

THE PROMISED LIFE

God created all of us. We're family. Family stand and fight together to win. (Take a look back at the chapter, "Willing to Have a Supportive Team." The word "family" can be applied there, too). John 10:10 reveals that Jesus came to give us an abundant life. Victory is already ours. However, this victory only comes as we trust God, walk in faith, and stand.

For everyone born of God is victorious and overcomes the world; and this is the victory that has conquered and overcome the world – our [continuing, persistent] faith [in Jesus the Son of God].
1 John 5:4-5 AMP

Knowing that God is for us, with us, and in us should cause us to say "bring it on" and walk in confidence. That's what David did when he came against the giant Goliath (1 Samuel 17). David took his shepherd's staff, placed five smooth stones in the pocket of his shepherd's pack, and approached Goliath with his sling in his hand. Picture this: Goliath has a bronze helmet on his head and is dressed in his armor – all 126 pounds of it. He carries a bronze sword and the tip of his spear weighs over 15 pounds. It looks like David is about to be squashed, but here is what David declares. He knew he had the victory before he even started the fight:

You come at me with sword and spear and battle-ax. I come at you in the name of God-of-the-Angel-Armies, the God of Israel's troops, whom you curse and mock. This very day God is handing you over to me. I'm about to kill you, cut off your head, and serve up your body and the bodies of your Philistine buddies to the crows and coyotes. The whole earth will know that there's an extraordinary God in Israel. And everyone gathered here will learn that God doesn't save by means of sword or spear. The battle belongs to God – he's handing you to us on a platter!
1 Samuel 17:45-47 MSG

Does this sound like a crazy person talking or someone looking to be killed? We're talking about a little guy standing up to a giant that was nearly 10 feet tall (depending on which Bible version you read). They both take off running toward each other when David reaches into his pocket for a stone, slings it, and hits Goliath straight in the forehead. After Goliath crashes face down in the dirt, David stands over him, takes Goliath's sword and does just what he said he would do: cuts off Goliath's head. The Philistines see that Goliath is dead and run for their lives.

What was so different about David that he could come against a giant like Goliath and say, "I come at you in the name of God-of-the-Angel-Armies, the God of Israel's troops..."? David wasn't intimidated or discouraged when Goliath said, "I'll make roadkill of you for the buzzards. I'll turn you into a tasty morsel for the field mice" (1 Samuel 17:44). He wasn't moved that Goliath saw him as "a mere youngster, apple-cheeked and peach-fuzzed" (1 Samuel 17:42). David took a stand and was confident in whom he believed. He walked by faith. He was not moved by what he was seeing or by what he was hearing. He had God's peace. As a result, God brought victory and received the glory.

God is on our side and wants to do the same for us that He did for David. We must be consistent and we must be persistent. We have to stick with it even when the going gets tough, and even when we may not feel like going. We are not like those who turn back because of fear. Psalm 23:4 reminds us that we don't have to fear. Do not stop pressing forward.

Pause Break – Pause Break!

We can stand when we know in whom we believe. It's like a child hinging on to every word of their parent. The child's parent says it and that settles it. Well, God said it and it's forever settled. Our part is to believe Him, not be moved by our circumstances, and stand. He is for us.

CONFIDENCE IN CHRIST

When you don't know what else to do and you have done everything you know to do, stand. Stand in the full armor of God and in the anointing of the Holy Spirit. Be washed in the blood of Jesus, filled with the Holy Spirit, and passionate for our God. Stand. When you can't take one more step, stand firm right there. God, Himself, is fighting your battle.

We're no different than King Jehoshaphat when the Moabites and the Ammonites, together with some of the Meunites, came to make war against him in 2 Chronicles 20 AMP:

Then Jehoshaphat was afraid and set himself [determinedly, as his vital need] to seek the Lord; and he proclaimed a fast throughout all Judah. So [the people of] Judah gathered together to seek help from

*the Lord; indeed they came from all the cities of Judah to seek
the Lord [longing for Him with all their heart].*
(verses 3-4 AMP)

*O our God, will You not judge them? For we are powerless against
this great multitude which is coming against us. We do not know
what to do, but our eyes are on You.*
(verse 12 AMP)

*He said, "Listen carefully, all [you people of] Judah, and you
inhabitants of Jerusalem, and King Jehoshaphat. The Lord says this to
you: 'Be not afraid or dismayed at this great multitude, for the battle
is not yours, but God's. Go down against them tomorrow. Behold,
they will come up by the ascent of Ziz, and you will find them at the
end of the river valley, in front of the Wilderness of
Jeruel. You need not fight in this battle; take your positions, stand and
witness the salvation of the Lord who is with you, O Judah and
Jerusalem. Do not fear or be dismayed; tomorrow go out against them,
for the Lord is with you.'"*
(verses 15-17 AMP)

In these scriptures we find God's people in the same place we
sometimes find ourselves, but God is telling them to "be not
afraid or dismayed" for "the battle is not yours, but God's."
And that's why we seek God and keep our eyes on Him. The
Lord will do for us what He did for King Jehoshaphat. We're
on the winning team. Now, let's take our positions, stand and
witness the salvation of the Lord who is with us. Trust God,
stand, and keep standing. Thank you, Lord.

*If you only look at us, you might well miss the brightness. We carry
this precious Message around in the unadorned clay pots of our
ordinary lives. ... We've been surrounded and battered by troubles,
but we're not demoralized; we're not sure what to do, but we know
that God knows what to do; we've been spiritually terrorized, but God
hasn't left our side; we've been thrown down, but we haven't broken.
What they did to Jesus, they do to us – trial and torture, mockery*

and murder; what Jesus did among them, he does in us – he lives! Our lives are at constant risk for Jesus' sake, which makes Jesus' life all the more evident in us. While we're going through the worst, you're getting in on the best!
2 Corinthians 4:7-12 MSG

Remember, we will be attacked. We may feel beat down and defeated. We may even get discouraged and depressed. We may feel there is no way out. But we must hold on, stand firm, and not give in or up. We must be confident in Jesus Christ.

I asked the Lord what made me so different from others who didn't seem as victorious with their battle with cancer. He said, "You chose to trust me." I cried. He saw what I didn't see. I was only walking in what He said to me. He was all I had. That's another good place to be; a place where we only look to and follow Him. We will never be disappointed.

STAND IN THE FACE OF ADVERSITY

For those of you who may have an unwelcomed visitor plaguing your body, know that healing and every promise of God is His will. For those of you who may be facing other issues, know that His promises have been provided for every difficulty we encounter.

Now, it's your time to take responsibility and get in the Word. Seek and search His promises. Don't place any limits on Him. Keep the faith and don't stop trusting God. Be led by the Holy Spirit and the Word of God. Keep on God's armor. Let His perfect peace calm you in every circumstance and give you courage and strength for every challenge. Now, continue to stand and leave the results up to Him. He has you right in the palm of His hands.

All is well!

CONCLUSION

Sickness, deliverance, legal matters, depression, finances, family matters, or whatever challenges you face can't stand against God. He is looking for those who will dare to believe in Him and take Him at His Word. What do you have to lose? He is who He says He is. And He does just what He says He will do. Nothing is too hard for Him. Don't give up. Keep the faith. He who promised is faithful.

Stop looking at your situations and circumstances. They change, but God never does. And He loves us so much. He said He will never leave us or forsake us[42]. Our all-knowing God knew that there would be a knot on my scalp behind my ear and I would encounter a visitor called Non-Hodgkin's Lymphoma. He knew the facts would constantly change and wanted to make sure that I was not moved by what I was hearing. He saw the whole orchestration, yet nothing took Him by surprise.

As I travelled down this road, I became more aware of my dependence on God. It appeared that death was looming but I knew my life was in His hands. Paul said in Philippians 1:21, "For to me, to live is Christ and to die is gain." I knew I would win because I would be with the Lord in Heaven if I died and could love Him on earth if I lived. Although I am not perfect, I did my best to live a life that glorified Him. My desire is to hear Him say on that day, "Well done my good and faithful servant."

You see, the Word of God never changes; it isn't moved by our circumstances. John 6:68-69 (AMP) reads, "Simon Peter answered, 'Lord, to whom shall we go? You [alone] have the words of eternal life [you are our only hope]. We have believed and confidently trusted, and [even more] we have

---

[42] Deuteronomy 31:6

come to know [by personal observation and experience] that You are the Holy One of God [the Christ, the Son of the living God].'"

The Lord was with me just as He was with King Hezekiah (2 Kings 18, 19 AMP). We both had uninvited guests. They came to discourage, intimidate and take us captive. Neither guest counted on us relying on the Lord. The Lord told me, "Do not be moved by what you hear." He told King Hezekiah, "Do not be afraid because of the words that you have heard." And He is saying the same thing to you: "Rely on Me and don't be moved.

There are no hard cases for God. When they say, "It is impossible," you say, "With God all things are possible." Don't give up! Keep moving like trucks on the highway going up a hill. They move slow but they never stop. Once they make it up the hill, they move right along. You're going to make it up the hill, too.

The battle has been fought and we are victorious. Jesus paid the price on the Cross for whatever we may need – healing, deliverance, finances, peace. It's paid in full – no lay-a-way. All we have to do is receive and then walk it out, by faith. What do we have to lose? Let's answer together...*Nothing*. Not a thing!

It is my hope and prayer that you've been encouraged to trust God and keep the faith. Everyone's journey is different, but God is always the same. Your journey may seem impossible, but *no journey* is impossible with God. Remember the One who said all things are possible to those who believe. Hang in there.

Jesus Christ loves us dearly and is the answer to all of life's circumstances. While a cancer diagnosis was a big surprise to my family and me, I am just grateful that I have a personal relationship with Him. He is mine and I am His. I stuck with the Truth and refused to be moved. At the end of the day, I chose to stand and leave the results up to Him.

If you have not made the decision to make Him your Savior and Lord, let me encourage you to do so. You can have His peace and your life will never be the same. I can't explain it.

You'll have to accept Him to experience it. He will walk with us every step of the way if we invite Him in. He's waiting on the invitation. You have nothing to lose when you're willing to die.

SOURCES

Chapter 2
Gallup, Inc., "How Many Americans Believe in God?,"
   https://nws.gallup.com/poll/268205/americans-
   believe-god.aspx

Pew Research Center, "When Americans Say They Believe in
   God, What Do They Mean?"
   https://www.pewform.org/2018/04/25/when-
   americans-say-they-believe-in-god-what-do-they-
   mean/04-25-18

Chapter 3:
The Alamo: 13 Days to Glory is a 1987 television miniseries
   later edited into a feature film about the 1836 Battle of
   the Alamo written and directed by Burt Kennedy

Gunfight in Abilene. Directed by William Hale, performance
   by Leslie Nielsen, 1967

Chapter 7:
Enough. Directed by Michael Apted, performance by Jennifer
   Lopez, 2002

Chapter 8:
Star Wars. Directed by George Lucas, 1977

A FRONT ROW SEAT

Written below are testimonies from the perspective of "team members" who shared Linda's journey.

"Would you come and be with Linda …. She's a strong woman but this kind of stuff brings people to their knees…" I was there and watched her response. She took it like a rock. I think what shocked me after receiving the news was her saying, "Let's go to lunch." We never spoke about cancer anymore until she came to let me know that she was stopping treatments. I was scared for her; it's my nature. She would always tell me, "Stop worrying, Worry Wart." My faith was strengthened as I watched Linda put her faith in the Lord. I've told others about her journey in order to encourage them. She handled this life crisis with such grace. She is such a living example of a follower of Christ and what it looks like to put faith in Him.

~ Jill Martindale

Linda called and said, "They say I have cancer." No parent is ever prepared to hear these words from their child. I was scared, crying, and went into a room and broke down. All I could think was, "She is going to die." I went home and told my daughter, Delores, and she said, "She'll be alright. Have faith." I never cried again. I prayed that Linda didn't have cancer even though they said she did. I was worried, but that soon left as I watched Linda carry herself like she didn't have cancer. She kept doing what she always did. I supported her decisions, to include stopping chemo treatment. She never said she had cancer. She always said, "They say," and never claimed it. She had faith and the Lord healed my daughter.

~ Lucille Harrison

Anyone who knows Linda would agree that she is very organized; everything in her life is thoroughly planned, properly filed, tabulated and on a spread sheet if possible. That is just the way she handles anything in her life. In 2007 when she was diagnosed with Non-Hodgkin's Lymphoma, she approached it with her usual "It's all good because I got this" attitude. Of course, I knew she was already planning and organizing how she was going to deal with it. So, she started her treatment but discontinued after two of them. I did not agree with this decision but there was no convincing her to change her mind. She had her plan, but most importantly, she had her devout faith and strong determination. Fast forward to the present: Linda has been cancer-free and in remission for 13 years. Her faith, positive attitude and determination allowed her to conquer and overcome this cancer. She is an inspiration to all and the world is a much better place with her here. Keep on planning!

~ Ann Bagley

I watched as Linda walked this journey with the utmost faith and confidence that all was going to be well. If she sweated, we never saw it. She was not visibly worried. Although it didn't keep us from worrying, I saw how strong her faith was and decided if she was confident, then I had to be confident too. Then she decided not to do any more treatments. For all practical purposes, I didn't think it was good for her to stop the treatment, so we waited to see what was going to happen. And then, she went into remission and we knew we should have been trusting what she was trusting. Linda showed me what faith could do.

~ Jill Hawk

ACKNOWLEDGMENTS

There are many people who supported, encouraged, and assisted me on my journey and with this book. Thank you, first and foremost, to my Lord and Savior, Jesus Christ. I am so grateful for Him being in my life.

For everyone who purchased this book, thank you for your support. In addition to investing in this book for yourself, a friend or family member, you are also contributing to HIS Prison Ministries, the ministry Fred and I serve to reach those who are incarcerated and their families in Alabama. In fact, all proceeds from this book will support that ministry. If you would like to donate to the ministry directly, you may mail contributions to PO Box 10025, Dothan, AL 36304 or email lwimes@graceba.net.

To Fred, my husband, quiet storm, number one supporter, and friend: you never said much during this journey but I knew you had my back. I am still speechless to this day as I try and describe your love and support. The Lord knew this day would come and He prepared you to be right there with me. The Bible says when a man finds a wife, he finds a good thing. I am so glad you found me over 48 years ago as your girlfriend to wife. I love you, my man.

I am appreciative for the care that I received from my healthcare professionals from Dothan to Birmingham, Alabama, from the front door to the exit. Each of you played an important role on my journey. I want to thank Dr. Gregory Bess for getting to the bottom of the issue, and my straight-to-the point oncologist, Dr. James Foran.

To my Team: Jill Martindale, Ann Bagley; my babies Shalunda and Christi Wimes; Wendy Davis; Elaine Bryant; and my Mom, Lucille Harrison (aka Coot): you understood what was required of being on a team (more specifically mine) and you didn't waiver, give in or up. Even my daughter's four-legged animal, Armani, was on the team as a trusted protector. No one came near me without his permission.

To Brandy Detter (my other daughter by the milk man – inside joke): Thank you for your unwavering commitment to Christ and for the hours we have spent together making sure I stayed on track. You will never know how encouraged I was as we sat, ate, reviewed and marked up drafts. You never tired and pushed me right along. I love you and as I've said before, "If I had to choose a daughter, I choose you. You are my Detter girl."

Thank you to those who prayed and interceded for me on my journey.

Finally, I want to thank Ebony Horton for her help five years ago when I approached her about editing my book. You encouraged me to continue to write and that I would know when it was done. It's done, Ebony!

ABOUT THE AUTHOR

Linda Wimes is an imperfect, ordinary woman who chose to not be moved by her circumstances and instead believe an extraordinary God for healing.

She was diagnosed with Non-Hodgkin's Lymphoma in 2007. Her recommended plan of care included six chemotherapy treatments. She completed two. She was diagnosed again in 2008 with relapsed disease and refused further chemotherapy. She received a small volume of radiotherapy treatment. Although she was told there is an ongoing risk of recurrence and is still given approximately a 30% chance for long-term disease-free survival, she remains cancer-free 13 years later and continues with her sense of humor ("a merry heart doeth good like a medicine"), no-nonsense attitude, and determination to not be moved by what she hears. Her response when asked how she is doing continues to be, "All is Well." She will tell you she trusted God and followed His leading. She will not say she is in remission. She says, "Jesus healed them all, and I am one of the 'all.' I will not leave here before my appointed time, which only He knows."

Linda serves Alabama communities in many capacities but the position she is most proud of is Director of HIS Prison Ministries, an outreach ministry that supports those who are incarcerated and their families. Linda has spent over 35 years doing life and serving others.

Linda and her husband, Fred, have two children and live in Dothan, Alabama. She can be reached at lwimes@graceba.net.

www.ingramcontent.com/pod-product-compliance
Lightning Source LLC
LaVergne TN
LVHW051409080426
835508LV00022B/3010